Teen Girls and Technology

What's the Problem, What's the Solution?

𝕷𝖎𝖇𝖗𝖆𝖗𝖞

EDUCATIONAL TESTING SERVICE

Teen Girls and Technology

What's the Problem, What's the Solution?

Lesley Farmer

Teachers College, Columbia University
New York and London

American Library Association

Published simultaneously by Teachers College Press, 1234 Amsterdam Avenue, New York, NY 10027 and the American Library Association, 50 East Huron Street, Chicago, IL 60611.

Library of Congress Cataloging-in-Publication Data

Farmer, Lesley S. J.
  Teen girls and technology : what's the problem, what's the solution? / Lesley Farmer.
    p. cm.
  Includes bibliographical references and index.
  ISBN 978-0-8077-4875-6 (pbk. : acid-free paper)—ISBN 978-0-8077-4876-3 (hardcover : acid-free paper)
  1. Teenage girls. 2. Information technology—Study and teaching. 3. Teenage girls—Psychology. I. Title.
    HQ798.F37 2008
    004.0835′2—dc22

                                                                          2007047698

ISBN: 978-0-8077-4875-6 (paper)
ISBN: 978-0-8077-4876-3 (hardcover)

ALA ISBN: 978-0-8389-0974-4

Printed on acid-free paper
Manufactured in the United States of America
15 14 13 12 11 10 09 08   8 7 6 5 4 3 2 1

Contents

PART III: TECHNOLOGY-ENHANCED LEARNING ACTIVITIES

Teen Girls and Technology

What's the Problem, What's the Solution?

Introduction

Quick! Picture a techie. Is the person a male? Is the person Anglo? Is the person a grown-up? Is the person using a computer? The White male nerd at a computer monitor continues to be the technology expert stereotype, even for teenage girls. That stereotype does not appeal to those girls, even as a date prospect.

Who is likely to be the most techie in reality? A middle school Japanese girl with cute techwear gizmos dangling off her body, she is busy IMing and taking pictures with her girl pals using her cell phone. Technology is an integral part of her lifestyle, not a separate "box" in her day (Yang, 2004). Now *that* picture might entice more U.S. girls, but the majority of them do not know about their Asian counterpart techno-girls. Fewer still seem to realize that their current interests and experiences will help shape their future—and that technology comprises part of the majority of jobs *now* as well as in the future.

With all the talk about the millennial generation and its tech-savviness, it is all too easy for adults to assume that these young people need little instruction or encouragement in using technology. The reality is much more nuanced. The telephone is still the technology of choice for teens. Nine-tenths of teens are wired, but almost half seldom use the Internet. While the majority of telecommunicators are now female, they remain underrepresented in technology careers (Silverman & Pritchard, 1999). Indeed, not every teenager embraces technology, sometimes because of poverty, but other times because of negative perceptions about technology (Children's Partnership, 2000).

One of the populations that is at risk in terms of technology use is teenage girls. As elementary students, girls tend to use computers and other technologies similarly to the way boys interact with technology, but in middle school that picture changes. In mixed-sex settings, girls will often let boys take the lead, and girls are less likely to take high school technology-related courses. Similarly,

1

girls are less likely than boys to take the math and science courses needed to major in technology in college (Hackbarth, 2001). As a result, girls are disadvantaged in life, and society does not benefit from their full potential.

Why do such behavior and attitude changes occur? It's not just a girl's hormones. Rather, societal attitudes and pressures send mixed messages to young women. The conditions for learning and practicing technology change. Girls react to these signals at the same time that they have to deal with their own developmental changes. In short, girls are social, and their society needs to nurture rather than stifle their technology interests and capacities. Indeed, technology should be used as a means for empowering teenage girls to become their best and fullest selves.

This book explores the realities and possibilities of technology engagement by teenage girls and calls on adults in the community to address these issues effectively.

The first part of the book details the universe of today's teenage girls and the role that technology plays in their social and academic lives. It also points out the societal realities that can impact girls' use of technology, often limiting girls' futures.

The second part of the book posits elements for success. It takes the entire community to systematically address this issue, from caring adults and engaging resources to positive learning environments and motivating activities. The chapters detail these essential factors, noting that the developmental issues of the girls should take center stage.

The third part of the book provides school-based and community-based engaging learning activities that adults can use with teenage girls to help them gain technological skills, as well as reframe technology use as a lifelong tool. Each topic is based on teenage girls' current interests and provides a trajectory for thinking about scenarios where technology can benefit the community as a whole, as well as advance one's future.

In its 2003 study of technology's role within education, UNICEF declared:

> Gender analysis should therefore be a prerequisite for identifying and understanding problems as they relate to education, and especially to

the continued exclusion of girls from quality schooling. Gender analysis guides the process of finding viable and sustainable solutions to the problems of access, quality and learning achievement. (p. 1)

Since the 1990s, if not earlier, UNICEF has been calling on nations to address girls' education. The American Association of University Women decried the lack of technology engagement by girls in 1992 and again in 2000. The cycle of inequity can and should stop. Now. This book can help.

PART I

TEEN GIRLS' TECH REALITY

Chapter 1

What's the Situation?

In the 21st century, it may seem absurd to address gender equity in the realm of technology. The majority of telecommunicators are now female; girls use the Internet more for education and communication than boys, while boys use it more for entertainment. Even though more girls than boys use e-mail and create web pages, the world of technology remains largely a male domain. Such is the perspective of girls—and they show little interest in joining that testosterone bastion. It should be noted that each girl brings her own personality, background, experiences, and values to the table, so no one picture can capture the variety of teenage girls. Nevertheless, generalities about gender trends have been shown to be valid. This chapter details how teenage girls currently view and use technology from a developmental point of view.

THE DEVELOPMENTAL WORLD OF FEMALES

Sugar and spice and everything nice? Well, that's not really what little girls are made of. There's probably more spice than anything else, although society reinforces the sugar more. The differences between boys and girls reflect as much nurture as nature, although even in the womb, male brains are larger and more rigid than those of girls.

Male right brains, where abstract thinking and sequencing dominate, are thicker than girls, although females tend to have thicker left brains, which impact image and holistic thinking. Girls' brain hemispheres are more connected than boys, so their brains are more coordinated (Sousa, 2001). When crises occur, the lower part of boys' brains dominates: fight or flight. In contrast, girls' upper thinking brain dominates in such cases, which may explain why girls tend to take fewer risks (Moir & Jessel, 1991). Because of

7

these differences, boys respond better to things and girls respond better to people. Girls have better directional hearing and boys have better spatial ability. Boys tolerate more noise, and girls hear more nuances. Girls have better visual memory, and they multitask better than boys do.

Developmentally, girls develop language skills earlier, and boys flex their already greater muscle more. Not surprisingly, girls tend to play more verbal games, and boys play more physical games (Pellegrini, Keto, Blatchford, & Baines, 2002). Similarly, boys play out their emotions through action while girls use words. Unfortunately, because girls tend not to play with spatially manipulated toys as much as boys, they are less prepared to succeed later with mechanical and spatial challenges (Moir & Jessel, 1991). In terms of emotional development, even as early as the primary grades, boys are better able than girls to separate emotion from reason. On the other hand, by sixth grade, boys are more likely to take aggressive action to solve problems. Interestingly, primary boys are more rule bound than their female peers; by their teenage years, though, boys rebel more against those rules than do girls (Gurian & Henley, 2001).

The onset of puberty signals the greatest gender-linked developments. Body image becomes more important, and both sexes can be embarrassed by—and awkward about—their changing bodies. However, their peers associate different connotations with those changes; early-maturing boys are usually granted higher status and more popularity, while girls are often embarrassed and harassed. Girls tend to increase their self-consciousness and lose their self-esteem, particularly because they are more conscious of peer and societal expectations about increasingly rigid body images and behaviors (Orenstein, 1994; Pipher, 1994). In cultures where gender roles are more defined and validated, such esteem "dips" are less pronounced; for instance, African American girls gain social power in adolescence, and Latinas' quinceañera rite validates womanhood. Nevertheless, those same roles can limit girls' potential if they do not fit the norm (American Association of University Women, 1992). These gendered differences also impact learning in that girls are routinely discouraged from registering for advanced courses in male-associated domains such as the "hard" sciences; those girls who persist in taking these courses often find themselves a distinct minority and may feel out of place. Even the stereotype of male dominance or achievement in such courses can impact how well girls perform because they—and their teachers— unconsciously play out the "predestined" attributions (Brownlow, Jacobi, & Rogers, 2000).

Sex differences also affect learning; school is a different experience for boys and girls (Black, 1995). For example, because beginning reading requires both sides of the brain, girls are, again, at an advantage. On the other hand, by third grade, math reasoning skills showcase boys' natural lead (Gurian & Henley, 2001). In terms of learning overall, girls tend to be concrete experiential learners, while boys favor abstract conceptualization, the latter being the main instructional approach in formal education. Girls tend to approach new learning more cautiously and reflectively than boys. Because of their more split-brain hemispheres, boys can separate their emotions from their reason, so they can be more field-independent, abstract learners, which is favored in schools. Similarly, girls tend to think more about the relative quality of ideas and their interrelationships. Boys tend to be more individualistic, competitive learners, while girls prefer collaborative work. Boys focus more on the product, while girls focus on the process. Because girls develop earlier than boys overall, their bodies assimilate learning faster. Not only does it take more time for boys to learn, but their attention span is shorter and they need more attention than girls. Girls enjoy school more and work harder than boys. Rather than follow and worry about rules and authority, boys balk at them. As a result, girls tend to get higher grades in school (Black, 1995; Philbin & Meier, 1995). Because of societal messages and poor advice, girls tend to take fewer technology-relevant courses in high school, thus limiting their options in college.

Gendered roles remain a significant part of human development and self-identity. It starts at birth through identification with adult role models. Girls bond with their mothers, which is a direct connection. Although boys also bond naturally with their mothers, they transition to their fathers as they realize the impact of sex-linked traits. Fortunately for boys, male traits are often more highly valued than female traits, which facilitates and reinforces male bonding. Nevertheless, even as toddlers, children gravitate to same-sex play, even though consciously unaware of their own gender identity. A second method of developing gender role is experiential: Children behave in certain ways, and others react to them, often telling them what is appropriate or not. For instance, when little boys put on Mommy's jewelry or lipstick, many adults will tell them that only little girls do that: "That's a sissy thing to do." These admonitions may differ depending on the person giving the advice, but nonetheless, a normative regulation occurs. As noted before, girls see that society often favors males, so they are more likely to work harder to learn supposedly masculine traits, such as experimental design and leadership. Because of their awareness and need for social acceptance, girls also quickly learn which masculine traits will not be tolerated in girls, such as aggression. As they mature, children balance their knowledge about gender with social gender-role expectations and self-confidence about their own standards and beliefs (Bussey & Bandura, 1999). In general, teenage girls tend to have less self-confidence in their own identity, so they are more likely to follow social norms than to follow their own passions. This is another reason why technology is given short shrift by this population.

A MILLENNIAL WORLD

Today's girls are members of the millennial generation, born since 1980. This newest group of people exhibits a unique set of characteristics, largely the result of societal and cultural changes. Globalization has led to fewer cultural distinctions and a greater common language (often based on music and television). This generation has mixed together more than prior generations, and its members are more likely to believe in equal gender roles. Nevertheless, they are surprisingly family oriented (Ousley, 2006).

Because of the ubiquity of multimedia, millennials tend to use more modalities and think less linearly. Although they can be surface oriented, they seek active involvement. Likewise, while their attention may seem short at times, they can also spend hours on some activity of their own choosing. While they seem to have a sense of entitlement and appear egocentric, they are very social and more tolerant than past generations. Nevertheless, they highly value authenticity and directness, and they want to make a difference in society. Although they can be very conventional in their thinking and need a sense of security, they also tend to be greater risk-takers and more creatively expressive (Leonard, 2003; McLester, 2007). Howe and Strauss (2007) assert that girls dominate this generation because of their approach to lifelong learning and management: collaboratively based, open ended, and contextualized. Increasingly, left-brain jobs are being outsourced; right-brain, high-concept, and high-touch jobs, which reflect female thinking, are in demand nationwide (Pinkard, 2005).

Millennial learners tend to multitask and learn by doing (Carlson, 2005). They expect to be able to make choices and customize their learning. They tend to learn actively, and they want immediate results; they are also less fearful of failure. In terms of information seeking, millennials are not intent on looking for the right answer; in fact, they tend to perceive all information as being equal. Likewise, the format of information makes little difference to them in terms of credibility. They expect instant information and feel comfortable performing several tasks simultaneously, yet they experience information overload (McLester, 2007). They are high communicators, although their formal knowledge of grammar and speaking may not be well developed. In fact, for most millennials, their overall scholastic goal is "good-enough" learning and intellectual "skimming," partly because they feel overstressed and partly because schools themselves do not emphasize deep engagement in learning (Carlson, 2005).

In terms of technology, millennials are considered the first generation of digital natives. The Internet, cell phones, faxes, bar codes, high-definition television, and virtual reality have always been around (Beloit College, 2007). A 2005 study by the Kaiser Family Foundation found that youth spend an average of almost six and a half hours daily using media, and in 2003, the Internet surpassed television as the medium of choice among teens (Harris Interactive and Teenage Research Unlimited, 2003). When EDUCAUSE surveyed incoming college freshmen in 2006, it discovered that over 98% owned computers and about three-quarters owned a portable music or video storage/player device. They spent an average of 18 hours weekly online, principally for communicating (Salaway, Caruso, & Nelson, 2007). Teens also use technology for entertainment (especially gaming for boys), finding personal information, and creating content and sharing it (Rainie,

2006). Because of such technological ubiquity, this generation expects information to be convenient and available all the time; for this reason, they favor portable devices. Likewise, they are likely to interact with a variety of information sources simultaneously (Abram & Luther, 2004). Basically, teens choose their form of media based on the type of activity: phones for immediate personal contact, television for news, video games for escape. It should also be noted that teens do not use media homogeneously.

In 2003, Harris Interactive and Teen Research Unlimited marketers classified millennial media/technology users into six cluster groups:

- Hubs (15%): heaviest Internet users. They want the latest information.
- Chic Geeks (16%): rebellious, urban, early technology adaptors with a wide social network. They seek the newest trends.
- Miss Insulars (18%): tech fringers. They check whether information is accurate.
- Alter-ego.coms (14%): heavy Internet users but unconfident. They prefer life online.
- IQ Crew (15%): highly educated loners. They want practical information.
- Now Crowd (22%): social, suburban heavy media users. They want immediate information.

Of course, just because this generation has been surrounded by technology does not mean that its members are tech-savvy, and many do not see a need to be so. Males tend to overrate their technology prowess, while females tend to underrate their ability. Again, the principle of "good enough" applies to technology use, which also reflects a "need-to-know" assessment and an ongoing prioritization of time management. Incoming college freshmen self-report that they know enough technology to do what they need to do, and they tend to think of technology in terms of the context: personal versus academic. Nevertheless, students think that their teachers should become more tech-savvy and that teacher instruction should remedy any technological limitations they may have that affect schoolwork (Salaway et al., 2007).

THE WORLD OF 21st-CENTURY TEENAGERS

What is the world of today's teenagers? Fast-paced and sometimes agonizingly slow. Crowded yet isolating. Exciting and scary. Full of choices and yet limiting. So many variables impact teenagers in general and in daily situations—regarding family, friends, school, community, socioeconomic realities, politics, natural and manmade resources—that it is hard to generalize about them. The 21st century is not an easy time to be a teenager. Defining moments and issues for these youth include 9/11, terrorism, and the war in Iraq. The period of adolescence has lengthened as more skills are needed to survive financially; on the other hand, teenage girls are experiencing their first menstrual period earlier than ever, thanks to improved health conditions. As more dangers and choices lurk, the disconnect between sexual and emotional maturity can have life-impacting ramifications. The increase in mobility has eroded community stability and family networks. Although it is wonderful that young people have more options than ever in terms of life choices, that reality can be overwhelming for youth (Children's Defense Fund, 2005).

Here are some other realities facing teens:

- A declining percentage of minors live with two married parents: two-thirds in 2006, down from over three-quarters in 1980.
- The percentage of 15- to 17-year-old mothers has fallen 40% since 1991, down to 21 births per 1,000, and has decreased by 60% by African American teens.
- The adolescent birth rate for females age 15 to 17 continued to decline. The rate fell by more than two-fifths between 1991 and 2005, reaching 21 births per 1,000 females. The 2004–2005 decline was particularly steep among Black, non-Hispanic, and Asian or Pacific Islander adolescents. The birth rate for Black, non-Hispanic adolescents dropped three-fifths from 1991 to 2005.
- The main causes of injuries for teens age 15 to 19 treated in hospital emergency rooms were being struck by or against an object (33 per 1,000), motor vehicle crashes (25 per 1,000), and falls (20 per 1,000).

- Almost half of high school students reported that they had had sexual intercourse.
- Between 1982 and 2004, the percentage of high school graduates who had completed an advanced mathematics course almost doubled, increasing from 26% to 50%. Similarly, two-thirds had completed science courses, again almost double the number from 1982.
- Over two-thirds of high school graduates enrolled directly in a two- or four-year college (Federal Interagency Forum on Child and Family Statistics, 2007).

FOCUSING ON TODAY'S TEENAGE GIRLS

This generation of U.S. teenage girls is probably the most diverse in terms of ethnicities, backgrounds, and experiences. Nevertheless, some psychological conditions resonate for most teenage girls today.

- Girls want to be a part of a group and develop friendships.
- Girls want to identify their own values and develop their unique identity.
- Girls need to feel safe to express their questions and opinions and need help dealing with stress.
- Girls feel pressured by others to conform and to succeed.
- Girls want a feeling of accomplishment, but they also want to have fun.
- Girls like to learn by doing and by connecting with other girls and adults who are teen-savvy.
- Girls want flexibility and choice in their lives, and they want to plan with adults to make things happen (Schoenberg et al., 2002).

Within this framework, an 11-year-old's experience differs vastly from that of a 17-year-old. In its study of teenagers, the Girls Scouts of the USA (2002) identified three subgroups: preteen 11- to 13-year-olds, teen 13- to 15-year-olds, and young adult 15- to 17-year-olds. Here are some of their findings:

- Preteen 11- to 13-year-olds focus on transitioning to middle school and fitting in there. They are starting to feel peer pressure as they are confronting a new level of risk-taking issues (e.g., sex and drugs). In general, though, they are eager to explore the world around them.
- Teen 13- to 15-year-olds focus on themselves as they experience rites of passage. They worry about their self-image and need self-assurance. They feel social pressure to behave in certain ways, which counters their need for self-expression.
- Young adult 15- to 17-year-olds focus on graduating and life ahead. They have more independence and responsibilities, which also add pressure to succeed. They feel stress and look for skills to help them survive day to day as well as to prepare for an uncertain future (Schoenberg et al., 2002).

TEENAGE GIRLS AND TECHNOLOGY

As millenials, girls have always lived in a digital world, watched cable television, clicked digital cameras, played on Game Boys, and "owned" virtual pets (Beloit College, 2007). Japanese teenage girls exemplify "techno-cultural suppleness": the ability to find emerging technology and then mold it to their own uses, sporting colorful cell phones so they can connect with e-mail icon "messengers," taking photos with blinking-light digital cameras that incorporate MP3 players, wearing tiny pink MiniDisc players with clip-on remotes (Mann, 2001). Technology is not a separate world; it almost serves as electronic wallpaper in their lives. As such, girls might not even realize the extent to which they rely on technology, even in the most isolated areas. Girls are digital natives, but just as someone who lives in the United States might not speak English, today's young women might not speak "techie." IMing does not equate with efficient online searching or digital data analysis.

Girls have a range of feelings about technology, but in general they can like technology as a tool rather than as an end, particularly as a social, communication activity. Girls and boys have similar attitudes about technology in the primary grades, but by sixth grade, girls self-report less positive attitudes about technology (Hackbarth, 2001). Both boys and girls consider technology to be a male domain, so when societal messages about gender-appropriate roles are foisted on pubescent girls, females tend to withdraw from technology (Christensen, Knezek, & Overall, 2005; Pinkard, 2005). Girls have been known to get home computers, try them out, and then practically abandon them in their teenage years (Coomber, Colley, Hargreaves, & Dorn, 1997). Interestingly, girls not only think that females are as technologically capable as males, but they also think that they use technology in more positive ways than boys (Thom, 2001). Nevertheless, most girls do not see technology as a personal career choice (Francis & Katz, 1996).

One gender-linked behavior relative to computer use is anxiety. About a third of the adult population experiences computer-related technology anxiety, with females constituting the vast majority (Brosnan, 1998). This finding crosses age and cultural boundaries. Several factors are involved: use of male characters and objectification of female characters, timed contests, perception of computers as math machines. When girls play computer games in public, they perform less well—unlike boys. Likewise, when gaming performance is used as a high-stakes factor in grading, girls tend to fail—unlike boys. However, when games are low stake and played in private, girls often beat boys. The main underlying issue is peer perception. As a result of computer anxiety, girls are likely to avoid computers, to harbor negative views about technology, and to feel less technologically competent. This attitude is exacerbated by the fact that girls tend to underrate their own technological ability and boys tend to overrate their prowess. Attribution theory also comes into play, which addresses a person's sense of control and efficiency. When girls are successful with computers, they attribute the accomplishment to the machine; but when they experience failure, girls blame themselves rather than the limitations of the technology. Sadly, these attitudes permeate girls' decisions for the rest of their lives (Cooper & Weaver, 2003).

Large (2005) synthesized several studies about web-based information-seeking behaviors, providing significant insights about teenage girls' attitudes toward and use of technology. Girls tend to use more words, spend more time viewing retrieved web pages, and jump between pages less quickly than boys. In addition, boys are more put off by a text-heavy web page. Girls are more likely to assume that Internet content is credible, and they are more likely to spend time with a parent searching the Net.

While girls use technology as much as boys do at school, boys have more interest and more formal knowledge about technology. Girls take fewer advanced computer courses and tend to underrate their ability relative to boys' self-perceptions (Pinkard, 2005). Furthermore, only 14% of girls took the Advanced Placement computer science test, and they scored lower than boys. Nevertheless, girls are more likely than boys to use technology for e-mail, word processing, and schoolwork; boys use it more for gaming (U.S. Department of Education, 2004). These gender differences relative to technology use continue through college and beyond, where females use technology to make connections in contrast to males, who use technology to demonstrate competence. In a study of gender differences and distance education, Morley (2007) found that females exerted more effort and made more commitments relative to technology and were more likely to ask for help. Nevertheless, males spent more time on computers and had more positive attitudes about digital libraries.

The social life of technology is often a completely different story. Ninety-six percent of Internet users age 9 to 17 do online social networking such as Facebook and blogging. Almost half of them visit such sites daily. Girls are the majority participants and tend to use these sites to reinforce existing human relationships. In fact, over 90% of girls use social networking as a way to keep in touch with friends they see frequently. In contrast, boys are more likely than girls to use social networking to flirt and find new friends. (Lenhart & Madden, 2007). The National School Boards Association's (2007) social networking study reinforces the above findings, stating that teenagers are usually careful about their use; negative online experiences are fewer than expected. Moreover, parents are much more involved in their children's online behavior than anticipated.

In short, girls regard technology as one aspect of their lives, but not a central interest or concern. Girls focus on their interests and needs, and if technology helps in their endeavors, they are willing to use it. But technology is not an imperative for girls. In fact, teenage girls still think of technology as a masculine endeavor, and because girls are so sensitive to societal messages about gender role, they are reluctant to cross those normative boundaries to explore technologies. Girls and society lose because of such attitudes and behaviors.

GIRLS AND GAMING

Gaming provides a microcosm of teenage girls' attitude toward and use of technology. Gaming has been a mainstay entertainment, but education has started to co-opt this pastime as a viable learning environment. In both cases, girls tend to be disadvantaged.

Many adults tend to lump all teens into the gaming generation, even though the archetypal gamer is a male in his mid-twenties. It is true that practically all children either play electronic games or know someone who does (National Institute on Media and the Family, 2001), but the connections might not be positive or strong.

Gaming has become more attractive as its elements have become identified as positive conditions for learning:

- Use of fixed rules, which are equitable
- Clear roles and expectations
- Representation of knowledge/content/event
- Immediate and specific feedback
- Ability to develop and explore new identities
- Sense of control, ownership, and investment in the outcome
- Active and manipulative environment; constructivist mentality
- Interaction between player and computer, as well as peer interaction
- Ability to reach a goal using a variety of routes and strategies
- Player effort, which correlates with success
- Authentic, complex, and contextualized contexts and tasks
- Blend of competition and collaboration
- Blend of cognitive and affective engagement (DeKanter, 2005; Deubel, 2006; Gee, 2003; Simpson, 2005; Squire, 2006)

Games are increasingly used in business, military training, and educational settings. Most of these games are intentional endeavors, which resonates well with males but does not reflect females' preference for casual games (Hayes, 2005). In addition, most games' motifs tend to be combative and competitive, which stresses girls. Girls are further disadvantaged because their gaming experience is usually less than boys', and they are not interested in complex hand-eye coordination. In fact, if it takes more effort to figure out how to navigate the game than to accomplish the content task, females are likely to get frustrated and want to walk away from the experience (Cassell & Jenkins, 1998).

The nature of the game, its characters, its storyline, its graphic features, its interactivity, its openness, its context, its incorporation into education, and its scaffolding all impact girls' interest and involvement in it. Girls prefer learning through personalized textual feedback, while boys prefer to use icons (Cooper & Weaver, 2003). In addition, each girl brings a unique set of values and experiences that shape her interaction with each game, so each game and each context has to be considered when assessing its effectiveness, particularly within a formal educational setting. Nevertheless, before educators (be they in academic institutions or human resource departments) jump wholeheartedly into the world of gaming, they need to ascertain the interests and capabilities of teenage girls and then set up the conditions for learning that will take advantage of girls' proclivities (Hayes, 2005).

Chapter 2

What's the Problem?

The 2000 report of the American Association of University Women on girls and technology found that girls were not technophobic; rather, they did not like the computer *culture*. They found programming to be boring, they didn't like the nature of most computer games, and they saw few positive adult female role models. Additionally, family and social pressures on pubescent girls start to affect technology access and use. The school culture is not much better. Technology-enhanced projects are gender neutral or more male oriented. Girls are sometimes discouraged from taking advanced math, science, or tech courses. Girls lack information about the impact of technology on career opportunities, salaries, and promotions. Thus, girls tend to classify all tech jobs as masculine. This chapter explains many of the reasons that girls tend not to embrace technology, particularly in terms of their development and their attitudes about their futures.

SOCIETAL MESSAGES

In elementary school, technology interest and capability is generally gender equitable. Girls tend to enjoy and succeed more with text-based technology, while boys dominate in mechanical technologies, but they spend about the same amount of time overall with—and have similar attitudes about—technology. The main differences in children's technological ability arise from practice, so given equal access time to practice, gender discrepancies disappear. Most importantly, teacher experience and technological skills, combined with technology-enhanced curricular projects, optimize student learning (Hackbarth, 2001).

However, as girls approach puberty, their attitude toward technology changes, as does their technology use. These changes occur largely because of outside influences. Because burgeoning teens want a sense of belonging and identification with others, they listen intently to their favorite peers and mass media figures. With their fragile self-identities, they are susceptible to societal messages; on the foreign territory of adulthood, they desperately want advice at the same time that they are forging a self-image. In this process, technology is usually assigned a masculine label, so vulnerable pubescent girls eschew such linkages. If boys are taking technology courses, then those courses should be avoided. If technology is linked with math and science, then girls are less likely to pursue advanced studies in these areas. If technology is equated with computers, then girls will choose more stylish portable gadgets such as cell phones. Unfortunately, all too many adults reinforce those messages. Adults and peers often link technology with tomboy behavior, steering young teenage girls away from such activities toward more feminine ones. Teachers and counselors may advise girls not to take advanced math, science, and technology courses if they think girls will not be engineers, not understanding that many service careers involve technology. Unless teenage girls have a strong sense of self, they are apt to follow others' expectations. When those expectations are based on biased, outdated stereotypes, they restrict a girl's potential.

FAMILY ISSUES

Families impact teenage girls' physical and intellectual access to technology as well as its use. Home is the first place that children might encounter technology. The good news is that families with children are more likely to have computers than childless ones. Other key indicators that predict family acquisition of computers include income, education, ethnicity, and workplace computer use; additionally, rural areas are less likely than urban ones to have Internet connectivity (U.S. Department of Commerce, 2004). Sadly, the same families that have less technology access tend to have fewer assets in general, so their daughters are at a more severe disadvantage. Furthermore, families are more likely to buy a computer for their sons than for their daughters. In families that have computers, fathers are more likely to use computers than mothers, although this picture is beginning to change (Bain & Rice, 2006; Compaine, 2001; Jennings, 2000).

Poor, at-risk teenage girls are the most disadvantaged relative to technology. Their families are least likely to own a computer or to model technology use. Interestingly, more than 99% own a television, and poorer youth spend more time watching it than do youth in higher-income families (Kaiser Family Foundation, 2005). Economic realities often require girls to start work at an earlier age or to take care of the rest of the family because parents need to work whatever hours they can. Parents may be less well educated, so their daughters may need remediation, which might well take the shape of drill-and-kill technology rather than open-ended technologies reserved for gifted and talented student creations. These girls may find their career technological skills limited to using bar code scanners and electronic cash registers (Weinman & Haag, 1999).

SOCIAL ISSUES

Technology is a mainstay for Americans: from birth to death, from setting the alarm clock and the coffeemaker before bed, from nanotechnology to astrophysics. Because of technology, the world is more interconnected than ever. Economic and social activities rely on information and communication technologies. Knowledge is ever flowing, and social interactions seem weblike (Daniel, 2007).

Nevertheless, concerns about technology abound. Does playing video games make boys more aggressive? Does Internet use isolate people rather than join them? Does technology dehumanize work? Has the web compromised individual privacy? Is nanotechnology invasive? Does outsourcing of technology jobs threaten the U.S. economy? What about fair treatment of the laborers who put together computer systems? Does technology use of petroleum products fuel the energy crisis? Teenage girls worry about the dark side of technology and generally feel that they have little control in these matters; they tend to flee from—rather than fight about—the issues (Brunner & Bennett, 1997).

Girls' problematic attitudes about technology become critical in the adolescent years, although they start earlier. Additionally, the social pressures on pubescent girls start to affect technology access and use (Center for Media Literacy, 2007; Eckes & Trautner, 2000; Jenkins, 1992).

ECONOMIC ISSUES

Both in terms of consumerism and production, the economics of technology impacts teenage girls—and targets them.

Technology marketers are beginning to appreciate the economic value of teenage girls. In trendsetting Japan, ads target girl gamers to buy Nintendo DSs for Mother's Day. Accessories for games can cost over $100, but teenage Japanese girls who want to stylize their gadgets lay out the yen gladly for gold lamé and bejeweled cases. Online shopping has become a huge market. Brick-and-mortar stores offer cyberspace "annexes," magazines targeted to females include online extras to gain more profit, "plus size" online stores enable ample-figured girls to shop privately without embarrassment. Do teenage girls impact the market, or are they the ones being manipulated? Often, teens do not think about those issues.

As for production, globalization and postindustrialism have given rise to the knowledge society, where intellectual capital has replaced material capital. Technology and service jobs now dominate. "Knowledge is innovation, innovation is quality, and quality is knowledge management" (Gilbert, 2007, p. 4). Collaborative technology plays a central role in this new economic reality, which draws on girls' ability to connect.

As a result, the need for more technology specialists and engineers has reached crisis status in the United States. At this point, technology industries are resorting to the outsourcing of technology jobs to experts overseas and lobbying for immigration requirement waivers in order to recruit qualified employees. Nevertheless, the percentage of females in these careers is disappointingly low: 11% in engineering, and 27% in computer technology and mathematics (U. S. Department of Labor, 2007). More startlingly, only 2% of U. S. patents go to women (Stix, 2002). Not surprisingly, businesses look around and see few women. Even though a glass ceiling sometimes persists, women in technology are pushing hard to attract teenage girls into the field. They know that girls need to plan as early as middle school, so they will have the classes they need in order to major in a technology-related field in college, get a high-paying job, and have a chance for promotion.

Even beyond the technological industry, the message is clear. American employers expect their workers to use technology, to use information, and to communicate effectively. As early as the 1991 SCANS (Secretary's Commission on Achieving Necessary Skills) Report, the need for employees to use technology was mentioned. With the advent of Web 2.0, the importance of social networks has grown. By using technology to share and advance knowledge, companies stay competitive (Nonaka & Takeuchi, 1995). Girls can blossom in this environment—if they know about it and prepare accordingly.

In the face of these realities, though, teenage girls choose not to explore technology as a career choice. In general, girls' image of technology-related careers tends to be very narrow. For example, when they hear about computer programming, they conjure up pictures of isolated cubicles, long lines of code, geeky guys, and caffeinated nights. Technology jobs are viewed as working with *things* rather than with *people.* Technology "feels" masculine, and girls don't want any part of it (Green, 2000; Koszalka, 2002). Girls also think that going into a technology-related job requires a whole-hearted commitment to technology; they do not realize that healthy skepticism about technology can be an asset in the field (Brunner & Bennett, 1997). Girls see few women role models, although this picture is happily changing as assertive, fun-loving girl techies in their twenties are mentoring their younger sisters (e.g., www. webgrrls.com/). The fact of the matter is, girls don't even see technology as part of any job. Particularly if teachers do not weave real-life technology aspects into the curriculum and career counselors do not show how technology preparation is needed for most futures, girls will remain ignorant of technology's economic pervasiveness and impact.

GOVERNMENT ISSUES

In the United States, governmental entities depend on technology in order to operate and provide services. Indeed, the big push in government today is convergence, with information technology playing a central role. e-Government is a significant part of the federal management agenda and is increasing its budget for information technology material and human resources. The Department of Homeland Security, with its coordinated security system, relies heavily on technology. Even voting has become electronic. Here is a growing list of governmental areas using technology (library.govtech.net/):

- E-Government: forms, groupware, portals, e-procurement, supply-chain management, work-flow management
- Policy: telecommunications, database management, document archiving
- Privacy: employee files, privacy rights, computer crime
- Security: authentification, data encryption and security, disaster planning and recovery, IP (internet protocol), telecommunications security
- Telecommunications: broadband and carrier systems, hardware, services
- Transportation: global information and positioning systems, imaging software, data visualization and data mining
- Workforce: human resource management and services, software, recruitment, staffing, training, work environment

Realizing the need for more tech-savvy government employees, as well as wanting to improve employment rates in general, the Department of Labor sponsors initiatives to help train information technology (IT) professionals. Government technology initiatives such as e-rate help subsidize Internet connectivity expenses for libraries and schools, to some extent because public information about government agencies has largely been digitized (Chao, 2002). People without Internet access may have difficulty finding out what services they are eligible to use.

To a limited degree, the government is targeting females in this push for technology. Agencies such as the National Science Foundation offer educational institutions substantial grants to develop programs that attract and prepare young women to enter science, mathematics, engineering, and technology fields. Government agencies are starting to create websites aimed at girls; the most often cited one is www.girlpower.gov, developed by the

U. S. Department of Health and Human Services. Probably the most impactful work relative to technology preparation is being done by the Department of Education, but its focus seems to be gender neutral.

ACADEMIC ISSUES

Education provides the main formal basis for technology preparation, and each of its elements influences girls' experiences in technology. Even though most school districts have technology standards, accountability is less certain. Likewise, teacher incorporation of technology remains uneven.

Stakeholder Perspectives

A coalition of businesses and organizations, the CEO Forum on Education and Technology (2001), has produced a series of reports on technology and students, asserting that technology can impact students' achievement and prepare them for succeeding in the 21st century. Likewise, the Partnership for 21st Century Skills (2004)—which is an advocacy organization of business, educational, and policy decision makers—developed a framework for 21st-century learning. In this framework, information, media, and technology skills constitute essential student learning outcomes.

In response to an increasingly competitive global economy, the U.S. Department of Education developed a national technology plan in 2004. Built on the foundation of the No Child Left Behind Act, the plan states the need for mastery and application of new technologies, particularly in the areas of math and science. The plan notes the vast technological resources that can be used to advance academic achievement, such as online and virtual schools to complement traditional instruction in order to meet individual needs and technology management systems to enhance decision making. As a consortium of educators and businesspeople, the International Society for Technology in Education developed technology standards for students, revising them in 2007 to acknowledge the growing need for creativity and innovation.

In synthesizing research findings about the benefit of student technology, Lemke (2005) identified three significant strands: as a driver for change, as a support for academic achievement, and as means for more informed decision making. Volman and Van Eck's (2001) review of research found that information and communication technology (ICT) contributes to learning by offering environments that help students solve real-life problems, providing tools to manipulate information, facilitating collaboration and feedback, and connecting school with the outside world.

In the last decade, K–12 education has progressed significantly relative to technology. Almost all schools provide Internet connectivity, and over 95% have high-speed lines, although effective incorporation remains uneven. Many students create e-portfolios as evidence of their learning, and production tools such as camcorders and photo-editing software help students express themselves creatively. e-Learning, particularly for Advanced Placement (AP) courses, enables K–12 students to transcend the resource limitations of their school site to get the education they want (Bethea, 2002). At the same time, families and students are increasingly frustrated with the limited online access time available to students during the day (Parsad & Jones, 2005). Nevertheless, administrative technology use is expanding; school record-keeping is electronic, and digital data on student achievement are analyzed in order to develop significant interventions. The ultimate measure of quality, though, is in students' work being valued in the marketplace and in their own lives ("Technology Counts," 2007). If girls do not use technology by the time they enter middle school, they are unlikely to pursue a technology-related career (American Association of University Women, 2000).

Curriculum

With the advent of the No Child Left Behind Act, one would think that the school curriculum would be gender neutral. Furthermore, the enactment of Title IX (1972) was supposed to address gender inequities in education: "No person in the United States shall, on the basis of sex, be excluded from participation in, be denied the benefits of, or be subjected to discrimination under any education program or activity receiving Federal financial assistance." Nevertheless, the deployment of the curriculum and the curriculum choices that students make indicate that gender issues remain.

Typically, assignments in technology courses, as well as in physics and mathematics, tend to be gender neutral or focus on more male-oriented topics, such as building construction, engines, and aviation. These habits may stem from engineering: "the creative application of scientific principles to design or develop structures, machines, apparatus, or manufacturing processes, or works utilizing them singly or in combination" (Accreditation Board for Engineering and Technology, 2004). Additionally, most technology courses view technology as an end, not as a means.

Just as important, girls tend to shy away from advanced mathematics and science courses, which are usually required if a person wants to pursue a technology-related major in college. Girls still perceive the "hard" sciences and mathematics to be a male domain, although they are approaching gender equity in enrollment. Courses in advanced technology, though, remain solidly testosterone driven. As a result, in 2005 only 15% of AP computer science test takers were female (College Board, 2006), a steady drop since 1999.

Instruction

Studies about gender inequities have been reported for decades (Sadowski, 2003). The incorporation of technology adds another dimension to these analyses. In reviewing the literature about girls' participation in technology courses, Jenson (1999) noted that behaviors had not changed significantly in decades. She recommended stronger interventions, such as girls-only classes, that *do* increase girls' self-efficacy about technology.

Without special effort on the part of educators, technology inequities occur from the moment that teenage girls enter the room. Boys tend to control the technology; if they have to share a computer, they usually assign girls to use the keyboard while they manage the mouse. In mixed-sex classes, girls become more passive and subservient; while they are bothered by boys' behavior, they tended not to call them on it (Streitmatter, 1998). Teachers tend to call on boys more but need to encourage girls to participate more, particularly in technology topics where girls feel less competent (Kimmel, 2000). Furthermore, some older male teachers communicate outdated and biased attitudes about females in technology, making girls feel uncomfortable, patronized, or conspicuous (Haynie, 2005).

With greater technology access and use in society, many teachers think that today's students were born with a chip, wrongly assuming that these millennials need little or no technology training. In fact, teachers are more apt to moan about cut-and-paste reports than about students' technology inadequacy. Teachers' ideas of technology incorporation may be PowerPoint presentations, Internet searching, and word-processed reports, all of which could be done outside of class time. Some teachers feel that they don't have to address technology issues because they think students can do such activities at home, an attitude that may be fueled if the school's equipment is outdated, overscheduled, or undersupervised. Teachers may forget that some communities do not have low-cost access to the Internet and that some families might not view technology as a priority (Daniel, 2007). Girls more than boys have difficulty accessing digital technology, tend to spend less time online, and have other home chores that compete with computer time.

Even potentially effective technology incorporation may ignore gender issues. For instance, building on the popularity of social networking, classroom teachers are increasingly incorporating computer-mediated communication (CMC) in order to help students interact outside the classroom and between class sessions. Depending on its format, CMC also addresses the needs of students with different learning styles; some students prefer writing to speaking, and English-language learners can look up unfamiliar words and take their time responding to a question. In a meta-analysis of how gender impacts student CMC use, Li (2006) found that females' communication was more collaboratively oriented, while males posted more messages and spent more time on the Internet. Herring (2003) concluded that males dominate CMC and tend to be more aggressive.

Professional Development

Some of these problems arise from teachers' own lack of knowledge about technology and its incorporation into the curriculum. To optimize students' technology use, teachers need to match the technology with the level of learning complexity, degree of student engagement, and degree of authenticity (Lemke, 2005). Teachers' own educational upbringing usually did not include methods of technology integration, so most learn these skills on the job. Indeed, their education professors were even less likely to have had adequate preparation in instructional technology. At both levels, males were more likely than females to have been introduced to technology and to have explored it independently, so stopping the cycle of gendered technology incorporation requires conscious interventions and attitudinal changes. Furthermore, training in instructional technology training needs to focus on gender-equity issues (Scheckelhoff, 2006).

Not only do teachers need to think about technology-enhanced teaching and learning processes, but they also have to identify appropriate resources. Most teachers feel inadequate to select software and websites, and have a hard time believing that school library specialists have sufficient content and technology knowledge to select effective digital resources across the curriculum. As noted above, selection should be gender sensitive. On the positive side, most school library specialists are female, so they are usually capable of making appropriate technology resource decisions that support girls' interests. Whether school library specialists seek girls' input into such selection decisions is another matter.

WHAT IS THE IMPACT?

The impact of girls' nonparticipation in technology, negative attitudes about technology, and limited use of technology reverberates globally. When girls do not see their futures in technology, they are not prepared to major in technology-related fields and have a hard time competing in the employment world (Green, 2000; Smith, 1999). More profoundly, they have fewer resources at hand to make informed decisions and enjoy their adult lives. Hence, girls might not reach their full potential, and society cannot realize its full potential, either (Warschauer, 2003).

As the matter stands now, elementary girls' attitudes about—and use of—technology are similar to boys'. Furthermore, their self-conceptions and self-esteem are also similar. Their futures are open. However, when puberty hits, girls become more self-conscious and more vulnerable to outside opinions; their self-esteem can sink if they do not have a solid foundation of internalized values and skill sets—as well as strong support from caring, responsible adults. Stereotypes that masculinize technology will endure if not challenged. Pressured to accent their femininity, girls will opt out of technology classes in high school and be unlikely to major in technology-related subjects in college. Doors of opportunity start to slam shut unless a girl is very aggressive, a characteristic frowned upon by society. Those girls who *do* take high school courses to prepare themselves for technology majors will usually find themselves in a distinct minority in college. Furthermore, societal messages about females' inability to do technological work will nag at young women's psyches; even if they are smart and able, they will start to question their own expertise, and a self-fulfilling prophecy is likely to occur unless teachers provides positive support and encouragement. Girls may change majors, endure their current major in quiet misery, or happily excel if they are passionate about their work, self-confident, and connected with like-minded females. Nevertheless, for many young women, feelings of failure will mark their lives, and more doors of opportunity will close. Their futures will become limited even further. Those with a degree in technology-related fields are more likely to get jobs in those areas, particularly since so many businesses are begging for tech-savvy employees. Nevertheless, young female professionals will be in a male-dominated environment, exacerbated by stereotypical attitudes about females and technology. Few experienced women will be available to mentor them, and, in fact, may seek to push burgeoning female colleagues down in an effort at self-aggrandizement. With so few women in the field, supervisors are more likely to promote a male because it is customary to do so. Some women will stay in their field out of financial necessity or because they really love what they do; others will opt out and look for more satisfying employment. As women leave, their male colleagues will be likely to say, "Another one bites the dust"—old stereotypes will be reinforced once again. Females' futures will become even more limited.

Society suffers. Government, industry, and communities will not have the benefit of a feminine perspective on technology.

Technology will continue to be user-unfriendly and nonintuitive. The resultant fewer innovations will lead to stagnant corporations, less profit, and buyouts by foreign companies. More outsourcing will occur, which will frustrate American employees—and the unemployed. With less employment, less tax money will be paid. Governments will have less income and so will need to cut social services. People will be less healthy, less educated, less protected. Social unrest will rise, and the social fabric will start to unravel.

While this envisioned dystopia is somewhat extreme, the elements for its actualization do exist now. The impact of today's decisions about teenage girls casts a large shadow.

Chapter 3

What's the Solution?

As technology extends throughout society, its impact on teenage girls increases. Equally as important, how teenage girls interact with technology impacts not only their own lives but also the livelihood of society as a whole. When society does not encourage teenage girls to use technology effectively, it limits girls' futures—and the future of everyone else. The issue will not go away. Solutions need to be found in order to promote an equitable, equipped society. Fortunately, governmental and organizational stakeholders realize the potential and impact of tech-savvy females and have made important inroads to address this issue. Their recommendations follow.

INTERNATIONAL RECOMMENDATIONS

In 2003, UNICEF, an arm of the United Nations, developed a set of recommendations regarding the use of information literacy by girls. It realized the importance of technology in offering new ways to help people teach and learn: to access and manipulate information, to foster interactivity and collaboration, to connect the curriculum and the real world, and to address distance/rural learning issues. At the same time, UNICEF documented the gender-based inequities in education, with particular attention to the incorporation of technology. UNICEF wisely pointed out that education is socially constructed (i.e., the presence of other people and the environment as well as one's own experiences and values shape the learning experience) and that education shapes the context. Thus, when females do not get equitable education, they are more likely to be excluded and exploited; they are unable to participate fully in their society. In light of these realities, UNICEF made the following recommendations relative to teaching technology with girls in mind: use the web to engage teen girls, use other technologies to engage teen girls, and provide mentoring venues to engage teen girls.

The gender divide for literacy and technology is evident. The international organization Women in Global Science and Technology (2005) noted the following factors that exacerbate this gender gap: lack of time to access technology, lack of infrastructure in centers that females can access, social norms (e.g., family expectations, attitudes about females in technology, and social class), cultural constraints, inequitable education, lack of female role models, limited employment options, financial obstacles (e.g., equipment and connectivity cost, limited public access), and cyberspace sexual harassment and pornography. The organization recommended several strategies to overcome these barriers: measure the impact of information and communication technology on females, provide females with more access to technology, support informal educational venues, use flextime for education, develop gender-equitable policies, and support women's empowerment through technology.

The International Society for Technology in Education (ISTE), a consortium of major educational and business stakeholders, has as its mission: "Providing leadership and service to improve teaching and learning by advancing the effective use of technology in education" (2007, p. 1). With its strong belief in the benefits of technology in helping students achieve in order to keep globally competitive, the ISTE has established technology standards for students, teachers, and administrators. In 2006, it developed a comprehensive policy document outlining its core principles and its stance on federal legislation. Its basic premises are as follows:

- Technology should be seamlessly integrated throughout instructional design and implementation, which requires pre- and inservice professional teachers and administrators.
- Technology enhances data processes.
- National research is needed on technology-enhanced instructional design and implementation, and findings should be applied to educational systems.
- All students need robust and convenient physical access to networks and the Internet.

In its emphasis on equitable access and use of technology, the ISTE has gathered research studies on gender, which are available in their repository, the Center for Applied Research in Educational Technology.

The International Technology Education Association (ITEA) focuses on technology literacy as a tool for problem solving and innovation. The association also fosters technology careers. Accordingly, its 2000 content standards are clustered as follows:

- Nature of technology: characteristics and scope of technology, core concepts, and connections with other fields
- Technology and society: impact of technology on society, technology's effect on the environment, historical impact of technology, and society's role in the development and use of technology
- Design: elements, engineering design, and problem solving
- Abilities for a technological world: applying design processes and use, maintenance, and evaluation of technology products and systems
- Designed world: medical technologies, biotechnologies, energy and power technologies, information and communication, transportation technologies, manufacturing technologies, and construction technologies

For students to meet these content standards, the ITEA (2000) stipulates that relevant educational programs are needed to manage learning environments that facilitate technology literacy for all students, that students should be regularly assessed in order to optimize their learning, and that professional development should be offered to keep teachers technologically competent. The ITEA is committed to ensuring that girls get equitable opportunities to learn technology through training teachers.

The Gender, Diversities and Technology Institute, an international learning exchange, focuses on gender-positive education enriched by technology and advocates for gender-equitable economic self-sufficiency. To these ends, the institute develops programs, synthesizes research, develops publications, and facilitates communication. In its review of the work being done in this area, the institute advocates more responsive and accurate ways to deal with languages; Internet content that requires low-end literacy skills; and low-tech, low-cost equipment to access digital resources (Nair, Flansburg, & Hanson, 2003).

NATIONAL RECOMMENDATIONS

The 2006 U.S. Department of Education's national technology plan acknowledged the realities of students' technological lives and the demands of the society at large relative to the use of technology. Although it does not single out gender, the report asserts that students are more tech-savvy than teachers and that schools that do not meet students' technology needs will disenfranchise those youth. The report also calls for more student participation in this educational reform, which can be a valuable way to engage and empower teenage girls. Most of the recommendations for technology deal with resources and teacher training: the conditions for learning. The plan asks for greater leadership, innovative budgeting, support for e-learning and virtual schools, greater bandwidth access, increased digital content, and integrated data systems.

Within the Department of Education, specific offices target teenage girls. The Institute of Education Sciences (IES) provides guidance for best practice that is not specifically addressed in a single program or initiative. One publication focuses on encouraging girls to pursue math and science. While technology does not play a central role in this document, its integration within this academic domain is vital. The researchers state that girls are as capable as boys in math and science but do not perform as well in high-stakes, high-pressure tests. The main reason for the discrepancy is girls' sense of self-efficacy; as young teens, girls think they are less capable than boys and then lose interest in math and science. To remedy this situation, five major recommendations emerged:

1. Teach students that academic ability is open ended; all students can improve their skills.
2. Provide timely, specific, and prescriptive feedback.
3. Provide positive role models of women who are successful in math and science.
4. Provide learning environments that spark curiosity and foster lifelong interest in math and science.

5. Provide instruction in spatial skills instruction (Halpern et al., 2007).

In implementing these recommendations, technology can play a significant role by facilitating communication, collaboration, and hands-on learning.

The National Science Foundation (NSF), another federal agency, has led the way in governmental support for girls entering science and technology fields. As early as 1981, the NSF developed programs that broadened girls' participation in science, technology, engineering, and mathematics (STEM). Its priorities include developing partnerships to improve STEM education for girls, advancing teacher preparation and development specifically for females, researching gender biases in education and learning, and increasing technology literacy for all but focusing on girls. Some of the best practices that have emerged from its initiatives include a modified curriculum, extracurricular STEM activities, summer camps, bridge programs, mentoring professional development for educators and community leaders, and parental involvement (NSF, 2003).

Several national not-for-profit organizations focus specifically on gender issues in technology. The Children's Partnership has as its specialty economic inequities. It points out that children are impacted by digital technology; they will not *benefit* from technology, however, unless they have equitable physical and intellectual access to it such that they can use it meaningfully and productively. It also asserts that technology can provide new ways to solve problems facing youth. Therefore, the Children's Partnership (2000) set up an action agenda for the public and private sectors:

- Prepare all youth for jobs and civic life through access and training.
- Ensure that schools prepare youth to success via technology.
- Use technology to help underserved communities.

The organization itself has several programs; it also serves as a clearinghouse for technology-related policies that focus on youth's needs.

The North Central Regional Educational Laboratory (NCREL) developed an assessment tool titled enGauge, which measures the capacity for educational enterprises to incorporate technology effectively. One of the conditions for successful technology implementation is gender equity. Girls need to be comfortable with technology and be encouraged to enter technology-related professions. The NCREL indicators of gender equity include the following:

- Stakeholders who know about gender issues and work toward gender equity
- Multiple ways to access technology
- Trained teachers who design inclusive, technology-rich curricula
- Software that links to girls' interests
- Girls who actively participate in technology-enhanced venues (NCREL, 2004b)

Numerous other regional and domain-specific organizations have examined the role of girls in technology and have developed recommendations and initiatives to address this issue.

WHAT'S THE POSITIVE IMPACT?

If these recommendations are implemented, the dystopian scenario described in the preceding chapter could have a much happier ending. Fortunately, the speed of technology advancement and adoption facilitate technology equity. Telecommunication is linking the world so that people can quickly become aware of changes. With the advent of the $100 computer, even youth in developing countries can explore their potentialities. As different options are shown, boys and girls can consider new careers that transcend traditional gender roles.

As stated earlier, elementary boys and girls are exploring technology as part of the world around them, gaining skills and self-confidence along the way. And as girls reach puberty, they have to deal with developmental and social issues. However, with the effective incorporation of technology, they can become better able to cope. Cognizant of teenage girls' proclivities and concerns, adults can set up positive conditions for technology experiences throughout K–12 schooling, but with particular attention in middle school, by doing the following:

- Providing girls with more physical access to technology: more time and more hardware, including girls-only computer systems
- Providing working surfaces that facilitate group technology work
- Structuring physical access to technology by making students take turns
- Providing a greater variety of technology tools, especially portable ones such as digital cameras and small storage/play/recording equipment
- Enabling and promoting social networking tools: IMing, blogging, wikis
- Developing more opportunities for hands-on and collaborative interaction with technology
- Assigning authentic tasks that draw on girls' interests, connecting them with their world in concrete ways
- Tying career exploration into tech-related activities
- Encouraging girls to personalize their efforts and end products
- Offering single-sex groupings or separate times for training and learning
- Offering girls-only classes and clubs that focus on technology
- Providing social, physical, and cognitive space for girls to get support and to feel comfortable working with technology
- Ensuring that classes are safe environments in which to take intellectual risks such as asking questions, exploring options, and problem solving until one is successful
- Providing positive personal support and encouragement
- Providing positive, tech-savvy female adult models, especially professional women in their twenties who use technology effectively and collaboratively
- Providing more teacher training in technology, particularly taking into account how to engage girls in technology (McGrath, 2004)

As a result of these conditions, girls can be intellectually and emotionally engaged in fun learning tasks that have personal meaning in their lives. The atmosphere for such learning may feel a bit chaotic for some adults. Girls will be chatty and noisy. They may seem to spend endless time processing. They may stick animal decals all over their laptops. They will be more aggressive, asking more questions and demanding more adult attention. Boys will probably act out more themselves and verbally attack girls for being more technologically assertive, so more time will need to be spent in single-sex and mixed-sex groups devoted to interpersonal and negotiation skills. In general, educators will need to be more technologically adept and flexible, and they will need to be able to design and manage more differentiated instruction that incorporates technology meaningfully. The curriculum as a whole may need to change to systematically incorporate technology across disciplines. Additionally, the school community will need to model can-do attitudes about girls and technology, including collaborating internally and with the community at large using technological tools.

By taking the time to learn more about technology options themselves, college and career counselors can advise girls more effectively, strongly encouraging them to take advanced science, math, and technology courses even if the girls do not aspire to college majors or careers in those areas. For example, the would-be singer may later realize that her academically learned technology skills help her in cutting an album, promoting herself, and managing her fortune. In addition, counselors can match girls with tech-savvy mentors from colleges and the community as a way of providing ongoing and future-oriented support.

The community at large can also advance teenage girls' technology participation. Parents will take a more active role in their girls' education: communicating with teachers more, training alongside their daughters, and providing active support at home. They may need to supervise sibling rivalries more and may need to readjust their own interactions with their now more assertive daughters. Other community stakeholders—libraries and other public service centers, youth-serving agencies, businesses, and organizations—can collaborate to provide coordinated opportunities for girls to engage meaningfully with technology based on their personal interests. Community venues can also enable girls to make powerful personal connections locally, network authentically, and improve their own neighborhood. As in other environments, community members may be surprised at girls' sometimes fleeting interests *and* sometimes dogged passion for a cause. Empowered by technology, girls may ask questions that threaten the community status quo, such as "Why aren't there free Internet kiosks in public spaces and shopping malls?" Communities will need to be prepared to respond to teens' recommendations if they are asked to help improve the locale. Given a voice, girls will use that voice.

These same conditions apply to postsecondary settings. Faculty will need to check their stereotypical technology attitudes at the door and get more technology and instructional design training themselves in order to address the needs of a growing female collegiate population. Technology-related majors may be increased because of greater female enrollment, so colleges may have to strategize on how to meet the growing need equitably. They may have a hard time finding qualified women to teach such classes, so they might have to do more aggressive recruiting from business to attract go-getter tech-savvy female professionals and provide in-house pedagogical training. Teacher preparation and doctoral programs will need to groom more women to play leadership roles in technology education.

The economic and political world will have a greater choice of technologically prepared and astute female professionals. For their part, females may also become more discriminating about the jobs they choose and be more likely to "make the calls" regarding work conditions. It may take more lead time at the beginning for products to be developed, but they will be more effective and ultimately more profitable because they will be the result of more inclusive and holistic thinking. With more communication and collaboration, work teams will be more interactive, more flexible, and more responsive. Old-liners may well feel threatened, but with enough tech-savvy females networking together and supporting each other, a tipping point will be reached so that the traditional ways of working will be seen as dysfunctional and no longer worth the hassle. Companies and agencies will be able to focus on creative, innovative products and services, helping their own employees feel more empowered and productive as well as satisfying their clientele more. Along with satisfying careers, women and their families will be more financially secure, healthier, and better educated because they will know how to use technology to improve their lives. As significant contributing citizens, women will have more self-confidence and power to make political decisions to improve conditions for society. Everyone benefits.

The return on the investment in the technological lives of teenage girls can be immense!

PART II

ELEMENTS FOR SUCCESS

Chapter 4

The Role of Adults

Caring, responsible adults can provide teenage girls access to technology itself and information about technology. Educators can facilitate career exploration about technology that addresses girls' interests. As a gateway to information, library use of technology focuses on information literacy and research, steps that encourage lifelong problem solving and decision making (Agosto, 2004; Crew, 1997; O'Dell, 2002). Parents and community members can link technology use to personal and social change.

To maximize their impact, adults need to know how to work with girls as well as identify their own technological skills and attitudes. This chapter explains how adults can provide a community-based approach to empowering girls through technology.

ADULT STAKEHOLDERS

Who are the adults who impact teenage girls' use of technology? The whole community, from parents to police. Even before birth, a girl's experiences mold her access to and use of technology. Did the mother use a sonogram to check her baby's health status? Such an action reflects a mother's attitude about technology and her approach to child care. Parents continue to influence their daughters' technology access and use during their growing years through their own behaviors and attitudes, their technology acquisitions for themselves and their children, and their support of their daughters' interaction with technology.

In the sonogram scenario and throughout the girl's upbringing, doctors function as another stakeholder in the well-being of girls, from diagnosing physical differences to overseeing eating habits. A girl's health affects her attitude and behavior relative to technology in several ways: motor dexterity to use keyboards and other input

45

devices, ability to mentally focus on technology tasks, the need to use assistive technology if she has a physical disability. The doctor's tools also demonstrate the use of technology: diagnostic instruments, databases of patient records, surgical tools, and so on. Other health personnel, including public health agencies and inspectors, also make sure that the community is healthy and lives in a healthy environment; technology helps keep records and facilitates timely interventions, such as counteracting poisoning.

Other community and government entities also play a role in a girl's technology use:

- Recreation centers provide technology-oriented programs and keep records electronically.
- Libraries provide digital resources, coach patrons in technology use, and maintain integrated library systems.
- Social workers offer assistance for housing, employment, and healthy environments, which affect technology access; they also use databases of information that guide people to appropriate resources.
- Utility companies install and maintain telecommunications and power lines.
- Safety personnel such as firefighters and correctional officers make sure that communities are safe: for example, that technology items are not stolen, that public utility lines are not destroyed, that computer systems are not hacked into, and so on.
- Building code inspectors and other construction officials address telecommunications lines and power and make sure that safety regulations are followed so that technology can be used with assurance.
- Local government officials, such as mayors and supervisors, create and enforce technology-related laws and regulations.

Of course, public and private educational institutions, from preschool to postgraduate, incorporate technology in their curricula, instruction, assessment, and administration. Each person in those institutions plays a role that ultimately impacts girls' technology use:

- Janitorial staff keep facilities clean and operational; they also make sure that electrical safety codes are followed.
- Secretaries use electronic tools to manage records.
- Technology specialists install and maintain technology resources and services and help the school community use these resources efficiently.
- School library staff, parallel to their public library counterparts, provide technology resources and services and instruct the school community in their use.
- Health personnel use technology to diagnose and address health problems and to maintain health records.
- Reading and special education personnel use technology for record-keeping, communication, diagnoses, and interventions; their competence in assistive technology—and teaching others how to use it—is key for student success.
- Athletic and other activity personnel use technology for communicating, scheduling, documenting, funding, and assessing activities.
- Student services personnel use technology to diagnose and develop appropriate interventions, which can provide the conditions for using technology (e.g., study space, negotiating with parents about technology use, etc.).
- College and career counselors provide technological access to information about future options.
- Parent volunteers work with other school personnel to incorporate technology in the performance of their duties and link school efforts with home reinforcement.
- Administrators allocate resources and oversee personnel to make sure that technology is used effectively. (Farmer, 2007)

Likewise, various youth-serving agencies use technology for their own sustenance (e.g., communications, record-keeping, security) as well as in activities for youth. Typical youth-centered initiatives include technical instruction, homework help, content development, web design, videotaping, online activities, podcasting, and public performances.

Cultural and entertainment entities offer many venues for technology-enhanced experiences:

- Concerts attract teenagers with their increasingly sophisticated sound systems and special effects.
- Museums include information computer kiosks to provide information and online interactive websites to complement on-site experiences.
- Sports stadiums and fairgrounds incorporate electronic billboards and other displays to announce results and give spectators ongoing updates. They also take advantage of technology to provide an exciting and comfortable atmosphere: music, lighting, even heated seats. Behind the scenes, they use technology as other businesses do for productivity and communications.
- Movies and other entertainment venues provide online schedules, advertising, and ticketing services. They also track user behavior for marketing optimization.

Local businesses also affect a girl's technology access and use. Besides selling technology-related products and providing access to technology (e.g., Internet parks, public Internet kiosks), businesses routinely use technology to carry out their mission, and they expect their incoming employees to be at least comfortable with technology, if not tech-savvy. Increasingly, businesses are forming partnerships with youth-serving agencies to provide technological equipment and training so they can prepare local youth for possible careers with their firms. Even without those outreach activities, companies depend on technology to survive. From advertising to billing, from ordering stock to checking inventory, from recruiting to paying benefits, companies use productivity, communication, and specialized applications to make profits. Their customers might not be aware of how much technology is present beyond the sales counter and escalators: lighting and security sensors, ambient sound, traffic counters, pagers, automated temperature instruments, and so on. Increasingly, companies have an online presence to provide convenient shopping—and to track user behaviors. Since one of the favorite activities of many teenage girls is shopping, girls may well be motivated to use the Internet and other telecommunication tools to increase their consumer skills.

Local service and professional organizations comprise still another set of technology-related stakeholders. Besides using technology for productivity and communication, these organizations may help young people incorporate technology now and consider technology use in their futures. Several women's groups, such as Women in Technology (www.witi.com) and the Junior League, focus on empowering teenage girls via technology: online websites, virtual mentoring, and technology-related events. WriteGirl (www. writegirl.org) provides high school girls with individualized mentoring and monthly workshops led by professional women writers.

In addition, national entities also support teenage girls' interest and engagement in technology. Federal agencies, such as NASA and the National Science Foundation, create online content for young people and offer grants to educational enterprises to help girls get interested in and prepared for technology careers. The National Academy of Sciences developed an interactive website aimed at middle school girls: www.iwaswondering.org. Among its features are interviews with 10 female scientists. Likewise, the National Academy of Engineering has a website for girls: www. engineergirl.org. Engineering is a particularly difficult career to promote because few K–12 schools offer engineering courses; that field remains a mystery unless girls know someone in the profession or have some other connection.

In short, the local and global communities are full of stakeholders that use technology routinely, hope that their constituents use technology, and bank on teenage girls' technology use to sustain their futures. Their support of this upcoming generation of girls is in their own best interests.

CHECKING ADULT ATTITUDES ABOUT TECHNOLOGY

Whether consciously or unconsciously, adults' attitudes toward technology attitudes serve as models for youth. Considering girls' perceptions about human relationships, they can pick up subtle signals from adults.

What are the attitudes of adults today toward technology? In 2002 the National Science Foundation conducted an in-depth study of U.S. public attitudes and understanding about science and technology. Here are some of its findings:

- About 90% of adults are interested in new technologies. Those with more science and math education have higher interest.
- Fewer than 15% feel well informed about the use of new technologies, and about a third think they are poorly informed. Furthermore, people feel less informed now than they did before.
- Most adults learn about the newest technology developments via television.
- Adults who have home access to the Internet are more positive about technology and know more about science.
- Adults hold stereotypical images about scientists and technology professionals.

It should be noted that having gadgets does not equate to having a positive attitude about technology or technological competency. A recent survey by the Pew Internet and American Life Project found that some people use just a few technology tools but are very productive and pleased with them; other people, however, have cell phones, PDAs, and other equipment but feel overwhelmed by—and dissatisfied with—technology (Horrigan, 2007).

Adult attitudes about technology are grounded in their own experiences from childhood onward. Boys more than girls are likely to have played with mechanical toys and to feel more positive about technology. Girls are more likely to see their fathers rather than their mothers behind computers. Likewise, parents tend to get computers for their sons rather than their daughters, so girls may feel that technology is a "guy" thing. Even school counselors may guide girls away from advanced math and technology because "girls don't need math." These societal messages shape youngsters' attitudes about and relationships with technology (Kim, 2000).

Today's adults are probably the last generation of electronic immigrants (Negroponte, 1995). A generation ago, few K–12 schools offered digital technology courses or provided Internet access for students. Today's parents saw movies and television shows that pictured huge computer systems and reams of programming codes. Adults who link computers with number crunching (which is an outdated image) may link technology with mathematics, which is also stereotypically associated with masculinity. Adults may feel overwhelmed by technology, especially at its fast-moving pace (Leonard, 2003). Moreover, because today's young people are considered "digital natives," adults may inaccurately lump together all teenagers as technological adept, an attitude that can be embarrassing for the young person who does *not* like technology and may feel intimidated correcting adults, especially if that action reveals the youngster's own inadequacies.

Adults also have mixed attitudes about technology in the hands of teenagers. The image of the teenager's ear glued to the phone is a long-standing gag. Now teen thumb sprains from texting messages have been added to phone folklore. Routinely, adults talk about their fear of youngsters cruising pornographic sites and having online sex—or being preyed upon by molesters. Teachers complain about student plagiarism and cut-and-paste essays. The 2000 National School Boards Foundation and 2007 National School Boards Association surveys of parents, however, contradict these dour attitudes. Generally, parents think that the Internet is safe and useful for education. They also think that their children are careful about interacting with strangers, and they monitor their children's use to some extent.

Attitudes about technology can fall along gender lines. Many adult women still consider technology as the Other, something that has to be dealt with rather than enjoyed and controlled (Harris, 1999; Turkle, 1984). Only within the last few years have women led technology corporations; traditionally, females have had to deal with a very male culture in technical fields, which sometimes undervalued family time or social relationships. Fortunately, Generation Y women are finding their way into technology-based companies and holding their own; these go-getter twenty-somethings have strong self-images and know how to combine technology aptitude with feminine sensibilities. These same young women are often eager to collaborate and mentor upcoming teenage girls.

In any case, adults who interact with teenage girls need to seriously assess their own attitudes about technology. Even if they are not experienced with digital technology, they should learn more about it so they can better understand its potential. Some adults feel uncomfortable with change or with learning; they should acknowledge this and try to encourage young people who feel the same way to have an open mind. Adults who have experienced few or negative encounters with digital technology need to process those feelings and try to exhibit a more objective attitude in front of youth. Females tend to take fewer risks than males do; therefore, all adults should try to encourage girls to take intellectual risks and reassure those girls that adults will be there as a safety net. In short, a positive, accepting attitude that supports girls' intellectual risk-taking vis-à-vis technology is the most important attribute (Deal & Barker, 2003; Fine, 2001; Gilligan, 1982; Labaton & Martin, 2004; Laskin & O'Neill, 1992; Mackoff, 1996; Orenstein, 1994; Pipher, 1994).

ADULT TECHNOLOGY COMPETENCE

Of course, adults' technology skills and knowledge need to be assessed and addressed. While the use of tools, such as productivity applications and the Internet, is a useful gauge, it is only the beginning. Just as important is the purpose for using technology: communication, research, data analysis, instruction. Both approaches need to be considered. Furthermore, because technology changes constantly, is important for adults to analyze their skills in light of current trends rather than preconceived notions of technology. In particular, Web 2.0, with its social networking, brings another dimension to technology competence that adults might not have experienced. Several instruments can be used as indicators of technology competency:

- Regional Technology in Education Consortium selection of self-assessment technology tools: rtecexchange.edgateway. net/cs/rtecp/view/rtec_sub/74
- Net Day Compass online resources that can be used by teachers or administration to evaluate teacher technology skills: www.netdaycompass.org/categories.cfm?instance_ id=54&category_id=4
- Ottawa Area Intermediate School District staff technology skills assessment tools: www.remc7.k12.mi.us/oaisd/ standards/skills.assess.html
- International Society for Technology in Education online

technology assessment instruments: www.iste.org/inhouse/
resources/asmt/msiste/index.cfm?Section=NETS_OTA&CF
ID=1231757&CFTOKEN=21086283
- Microsoft technology skills assessments: www.microsoft.
com/learning/assessment/default.mspx

Of course, the ultimate test of technology is performance: on
the job, at home, or in other environments. Some of the skills might
be very specific to the job (e.g., data input for a company-specific
database), but most skills are transferable (e.g., the concept of a
database and sortable fields). Even a fast-food touch screen connects
to information processing and can be a powerful way to track user
behaviors and impact company decisions about supplies, budgeting,
and staffing. While adults should know basic features of technology
and be comfortable with basic aspects of technology use, they don't
have to become techies to help support teenage girls' interest in and
engagement with technology. Like other technology users, adults
can feel comfortable with specific technology applications, as noted
above.

Adults should think about their skills in terms of how they might
inform teenage girls. A CPA can talk about money management.
A geophysicist can focus on ways that technology can help save
the Earth. A mechanical engineer can mention how her skills can
be used to make "smart" toys. Adults also need to determine how
to share the information. Some companies do not allow visitors,
and some technology is proprietary information. On the other
hand, many companies and agencies have active teen outreach
initiatives, encouraging their employees to visit schools and other
youth-serving centers. One-to-one mentoring can be done in person
and online. Of course, doing so implies that adults are informed
about adolescents and are comfortable with them. In some cases,
that knowledge may be limited to the person's own growing-up
days, so such adults should probably talk with other adults who
can translate the relevant tech skills into teen-friendly parlance.
Adult tech knowledge can be transformed into engaging videos,
web portals, and podcasts that teenage girls can relate to.

Adults also need to realize that their life experiences and moral
compass give them a unique advantage when working with girls on
issues of technology. For example, girls may know how to surf the

Net quickly and communicate with multiple friends simultaneously, but they might not realize what is appropriate to share with other people. Likewise, a girl may understand intellectual property concepts on an intellectual level, but she may feel that it's important to help a friend by letting her copy her homework rather than to see that friend flunk. The following statistics from the Business Software Alliance (2005) show the extent of cyberspace legal issues:

- Nearly a third of youth think that it is fine to upload software on the Internet without paying for it. Teens think there are more laws about downloading software than uploading it.
- Teens are more likely than preteens to download copyrighted commercial software and other digital music.
- Teens are more concerned about getting a virus than getting into trouble with the law because of illegal downloading.

The moral imperative is the last part of the brain to develop, so girls still need help in dealing ethically with digital issues. For example, adults know that they should not hack into company systems, that they should not steal people's credit card information, and that they should not plagiarize. Adults are also more savvy about critiquing websites in terms of their veracity, reliability, and bias. They can offer consistent messages about the consequences of inappropriate technology use while helping girls develop coping skills that enable them to be critical evaluators and producers of information (Baker, 2007; Hobbs, 2007). They can explain how a spur-of-the-moment decision, such as posting a compromising picture on the Internet, can haunt one later in life. They can give advice on how to combat cyberbullying—and discourage girls from broadcasting malicious talk about others; WiredSafety.com is a good source of information. Of course, adults also need to model ethical technological practice because girls spot hypocritical behavior immediately and will dismiss adult advice if it does not ring true. Adults also need to offer opportunities for girls to be creative rather than to report back what others say. For instance, when teachers ask students to write a five-page report on a famous scientist, the assignment almost begs to be copied and pasted. Instead, having girls create a mockumentary about scientists in a given time and place requires deeper analysis and synthesis—and precludes plagiarism.

In short, a positive, accepting attitude that supports girls' intellectual risk-taking vis-à-vis technology is more important than whiz-bang technological skill (Deal & Barker, 2003; Fine, 2001; Gilligan, 1982; Labaton & Martin, 2004; Laskin & O'Neill, 1992; Mackoff, 1996; Orenstein, 1994; Pipher, 1994). Adults are access facilitators—and psychological safety nets. At their best, informed and caring adults can transform teenage girls' lives.

WORKING WITH TEENAGE GIRLS

In the final analysis, it's not about technology; it's about the girl. Technology is a means to help girls develop their full potential. However, teenage girls want to be treated as worthy individuals first. Their prior experience and knowledge need to be valued and leveraged. Likewise, girls' social needs are central.

Girls may also feel uncomfortable or intimidated by adult strangers. Usually, adults need to be "vetted" by established entities such as family, friends, school, or religious institutions. Indeed, for community adults who are unfamiliar to girls, their own legitimacy and "street cred" needs to be established if girls are to pay attention to them. Thus, mutual trust must be established first.

Here are some tips for working with teenage girls:

- Begin with mutual respect. Value and listen to teenagers.
- Get to know teens on a personal level. What are their hopes and dreams? What are their realities? What is unique about each girl?
- Model what you want to see. Share yourself.
- Motivate teens. Draw on their natural curiosity and interests.
- Communicate clear, high expectations in terms of potential ability and social interaction.
- Give them tools to succeed. Train them, and let them train adults. Provide timely, specific feedback.
- Offer a safe haven for self-development. Let teens fail. Provide a safety net so they can learn from their mistakes.
- Let teens plan, and give them choices. Accept short-term

commitment, and be flexible with those plans. Aim for concrete, immediate, meaningful goals and results.
- Build a sense of belonging and community, yet let teens be independent. Monitor peer pressure.
- Appreciate and thank teens for their efforts, and tell them how they make a difference. Let them showcase their work.
- Have fun! (Schoenberg et al., 2002)

It should be noted that empowering girls means negotiating control, which may be difficult for adults (Putallaz & Bierman, 2005; Underwood, 2003). As girls enter adolescence, they need to establish their own identity and seek more control. When their desires contradict their parents' or other adults', girls have to decide how to interact. Traditional stereotypes about teenage girls, particularly middle schoolers, reinforce compliance and "girly" behaviors. With lowered self-esteem, these girls might take fewer risks and squelch any interest in technology. On the other hand, as girls become empowered, they may act out more and test their limits more, making them less agreeable to adult demands. Girls want equal billing and growing responsibility. Of course, they also depend on adults to be responsible, too, and to "save" them in case they get into trouble. Additionally, girls want adults to "give them some slack" when they don't rise to expectations or just feel silly and childish at times.

As girls get involved with technology on a deeper level and produce meaningful content to authentic audiences, they feel proud of their accomplishments. With that heightened self-esteem, girls may speak up more on their own behalf, particularly if the adults in their environment are less technologically competent. Adults should take this change as a positive indicator, welcome the opportunity to learn from these girls, and share control. In terms of helping teenage girls develop their full potential, the benefits of incorporating technology as a way to strengthen young girls' ability for self-realization outweigh the discomfort that adults might experience.

Nevertheless, it should be recognized that not all adults want to—or should—work with teenage girls. Adults may have criminal records or merely have past experiences that preclude them from beneficial contact with teenage girls. That is fine. In fact, stakeholders need to be aware of such predilections ahead of time. In some cases, the problem affects physical proximity rather than intellectual engagement, in which case other means of supporting teens can be used: online mentoring, creation of applicable documents, or even shifting job responsibilities to enable teen-savvy employees to have more time to interact with youth. In short, *all* ages need mutual respect and acknowledgment of their values and behaviors.

ADULT COLLABORATION

Because girls value relationships and a sense of community, adults should collaborate to provide an inclusive community-based environment for technology engagement (Belenky, Clinchy, Goldberger, & Tarule, 1986; Hom, 2002; Hrabowski, 2002; Jones, 2000; McGillicuddy-De Lisi & De Lisi, 2002; Oberman, 2002; Rice & Golgin, 2004; Thompson, 2005). Adults can provide intellectual access to technology, venues for physical access, and psychological support. As noted above, tech-savvy adults can partner with less technological adults who work closely with teens in order to support teenage girls.

Community-based, computer-based telecommunication has a proud history dating back at least to the 1970s. The public bulletin board service in Berkeley, California, used neighborhood terminals. The WELL (Whole Earth 'Lectronic Link) grew from the *Whole Earth Catalog* phenomenon and provided a virtual community (Hafner, 2001). Some Internet fiber-optic companies offer neighborhood network services as a way for the community to publicize local resources and services; girls can become network content news gatherers and inputters.

With the advent of cable television, each station has been required to provide community-based productions, which offer a venue for locals to have a broadcasting voice. Some of these community-based enterprises work with schools and youth-serving agencies. For instance, video clubs for girls connect with local cable companies, providing training and opportunities to produce shows that can make a difference in the community. Girls Clubs and Girl Scouts now routinely work with telecommunications providers to train girls in broadcasting skills and provide opportunities for girls to report on community issues.

The Community Technology Centers Network (www.ctcnet. org) is a leading example of a national not-for-profit organization that partners with local entities in order to empower communities through technology. Among their initiatives is Youth Vision, which engages and empowers youth to have a voice in community decision making by exploring local assets using technology and then proposing ways to improve that community. In the process, teens learn technological and leadership skills. The National Youth Development Information Center (www.nydic.org), which is a project of the National Collaboration for Youth, supports youth participation and development programs, particularly for at-risk populations. One of their initiatives is Chat the Planet, which includes conversations between U.S. and Iraqi youth.

For decades, secondary and postsecondary schools have offered enrichment opportunities beyond the school year. Colleges are particularly interested in attracting talented youth before senior year so both parties can size up each other in order to make the best educational match. Corporations also want to match their female employees to promising teens as a way to recruit prepared young women. As the need for technical experts grows, the associated colleges and corporations are creating girls-only camps to explore science, math, engineering, and technology. These opportunities occur after school, on the weekend, and during the summer. Most of these camps focus on hands-on experiences that leverage girls' interests: creating models, building toys, creating binary bracelets, making cameras, exploring marine biology, freezing flowers, helping the environment, making games, programming robots, solving science mysteries, and building Second Life projects. In publicizing these camps, hosts try to cast a wide net, so they tend to avoid "geek talk." Instead, they emphasize fun, friendship, and safe exploration in a girls-only environment.

Leveraging each stakeholder's strengths, the National Science Foundation collaborated with the Oregon Museum of Science and Industry and the Portland Latino community to create the Latinas en Ciencia project. They provided training about the Latino community's cultural impact on girls' participation in science and technology, and then created culturally sensitive science and technology programs for the girls. At a daylong event, girls served as museum tour guides for their families (Furger, 2000). Similarly, the Puget Sound Center for Teaching, Learning and Technology started the Northwest Girls Collaborative Project (www. pugetsoundcenter.org/ngcp/) to engage teenage girls in science, technology, engineering, and mathematics (STEM). Involving a number of partners, this project trained and mentored partners, provided technical support, created and disseminated publications, and sponsored events about STEM programs for girls.

The American Film Institute's Screen Education Center works with classroom teachers to incorporate filmmaking and media-production techniques into the curriculum. Their website (www. afi.edu/) includes a student center with online seminars, virtual interviews, and a gallery of student productions. While the majority of interviews focuses on men, a few women are featured in different industry positions.

Public libraries routinely collaborate with other youth-serving agencies such as schools and teen clubs to provide programs that interest young people; developing technology-oriented initiatives for teenage girl audiences is a natural fit. Family-based programs offered by community entities serve as a natural way to provide the conditions for supporting teenage girls' interaction with technology; workshops on family use of the Internet, computer software and troubleshooting, and photo editing let girls be a part of their family's exploration of technology. Even simple projects such as school or agency web portals that include parent sections to guide family use of the Internet (including links to vetted sites for families and youngsters) benefit everyone. Similarly, librarians can develop online databases of local community groups that engage teenage girls in technology activities and services. On an administrative level, different types of libraries can collaborate to develop policies that support youth and technology, such as the Online Policy Group (www.onlinepolicy.org/research/schoollibrary.htm).

For these community-based collaborations to function well as they support teenage girls' technological success, several steps need to be taken (Gambone, Klem, & Connell, 2002):

1. Know thyself. All stakeholders need to know what they can contribute to the group effort: technology resources, training expertise, knowledge about teenage girls, physical access to technology, financial support, access to youth-serving

agencies, and so forth. They also need to determine their present and potential capacity to help, having identified what resources they would need to actualize their potential.

2. Know thy community. All stakeholders know something about their community, be it political, economic, or social. They should also identify what they do *not* know but need to know in order to help teenage girls relate to technology. As part of this knowledge-gathering activity, stakeholders should identify those groups that would have that knowledge and would be likely partners.

3. Know teenage girls. What are teenage girls' interests and needs? What knowledge and skills does this population have? What role does technology play in the local life of teenage girls? What social networks do teens use that can be leveraged in incorporating technology?

4. Match needs and services. Ideally, adult stakeholders and teenage girls should collaboratively brainstorm ways to identify likely services and activities that would attract and engage adolescent girls in technology—in light of available material and human resources.

5. Plan collaboratively. Mutual goals need to be set, and strategies to meet those goals have to be decided jointly and in light of each stakeholder's affiliation. Stakeholders have to coordinate their efforts in terms of structure, roles, communication, resources, and services. Simultaneously, stakeholders must look within their own entities to make needed adjustments in allocating resources, time, and labor. Employees may need training: in technology, in collaboration, and in working with teenagers. They may need to review and revise policies as well as establish joint agreements.

6. Evaluate continuously. Adult and teen stakeholders need to examine how well their efforts are succeeding. Are girls participating, learning, and having fun? What impact is the effort having on each stakeholder's ongoing work? How well is collaboration functioning? How are problems solved? Are the results worth the effort? Are activities sustainable? Is there a real sense of community? With regular communication and thoughtful negotiation, collaborators

can make timely adjustments so that short-term goals can be accomplished and long-term partnerships can continue to support teenage girls' technology empowerment.

THE BIG PICTURE

What's important? Meaningful relationships between adults and teenage girls, between girls, and between adults. Technology is the content, but community is the context. Both are needed. Likewise, both cognitive and affective experiences are vital. Teenage girls feel better about themselves when they gain and exhibit competence. Adults can help girls gain that technological competence in a safe and caring environment where girls can be girls and have fun. Moreover, they can help girls be their best selves: selves that demonstrate a joy in being one's self alone and with others.

Chapter 5

Technology Resources
with Girls in Mind

In some areas of the world, technology seems ubiquitous. The 14-year-old Japanese girl with her electronic wearables technology exemplifies instant access to technology (Mann, 2001). Most teenage girls in the United States can get their hands on technology if they want to. However, the range of available technologies depends on socioeconomic situations even more than on personal desire. The point is to provide equitable, appropriate technology for *all* girls— and to show girls that technology can be used to further their own futures as well as to entertain them now (Roschelle, Pea, Hoadley, Gordin, & Means, 2004; Rosser, 1995; Sanders, Koch, & Lerso, 1997; Saul, 2004). Furthermore, careful evaluation of resources is needed in order to optimize learning conditions. This chapter details these different resources and provides examples of initiatives that foster deeper thinking about technology use (e.g., www.bluejeanonline. com, www.girlstart.org/, http://www.siu.edu/~sistem/funlink. htm).

THE WORLD OF TECHNOLOGY

A variety of equipment is available to explore technology, from handheld computers to laptops and cheap desktops. Digital-related peripherals, software, and other products abound. Equipment to capture and edit still and moving images is becoming very popular—and is even available in many cell phones.

However, technology in schools for formal educational experiences does not equate with technology found and used outside the school environment. To a large extent, incorporation of technology in schools has come about in response to social and economic realities in the world. The Internet is a good example. It started out as a U.S. defense strategy: a communications channel in case the telephone industry was attacked in wartime. Its use was broadened to include researchers, partly because advances in the technology needed the top minds. The widespread adoption and commercialization of the Internet are less than a generation old. Traditionally, K–12 education has been as likely to be influenced by the local community as by universities. Quite frankly, K–12 education has a conservative bent, as it seeks to identify and transfer lasting knowledge rather than flash-in-the-pan cultural fads. Generally, tools need to be tested and deemed cost-effective and learning-effective before schools invest their money and effort in acquiring and using them.

The impact of this reality is that many teenage girls use digital technology not commonly used in schools, such as MP3 players. Their technology skills, such as thumb-typing, do not equate with the technological competence sanctioned by formal education. If the outside world is a major driving force for educational adaptation, and yet education does not respond (e.g., preventing student e-mail activity), teenage girls might well question one or the other entity, and school may lose out. Already, students separate school from real life, be it reading for class versus reading for pleasure (which does not speak well for formal education) or school PowerPoint presentations versus interactive virtual social networking.

Fortunately, education and technologies occur everywhere and anytime. Rather than isolating or discounting technologies, adults and girls can approach technology as a way of life. Different technologies and their uses are situationally contextualized but may be considered in new contexts or for new purposes. This approach is actually a saving grace for school systems, which already feel overburdened with responsibilities for the well-being and preparation of young people. Bridging school with the rest of students' environments by acknowledging global technological realities and pointing out the need for youth to be engaged in the community's use of technologies affirm the roles of formal and information education and educators. Ultimately, in identifying appropriate technology resources for teenage girls, adults need to consider what works for girls and also what advances their technical skill with the future in mind.

HARDWARE

Gadgets. When people think of technology, "things" are what usually come to mind. In helping teenage girls start to think consciously about technology and its role in their lives, adults can ask girls to brainstorm all the technology that they currently use. Girls may forget to mention hair dryers, refrigerators, eyelash curlers, or ballpoint pens, to name a few. Even narrowing down the list to digital technology reveals the ubiquity of technology in most parts of the United States. Today's presence of technology resembles wallpaper: a background that most people ignore.

The adult world has taken notice of teenagers' buying power and influence, and is increasingly targeting teens for technology products, be it hardware, software, Internet, or tech accessories. Although boys still remain the principal teenage hardware client, adults see the growing potential of teenage girls as a target audience for technology. Unfortunately, their marketing efforts tend to reinforce societal stereotypes of girls: pink tech products, software, and websites focusing on appearance and romance, and advertisements that giggle rather than empower. Mattel started over a decade ago with Barbie pink computers and branded software. Justice brand clothing advertises girly gadgets in pastel colors: calculators, handheld games, phones, digital media players, and cameras.

The tech industry knows that girls like fun gadgets, such as T-Mobile's enhanced SideKick cell phone, because of the camera, communication, and music player features (and vinyl skins) associated with it. Remember the Tamagotchi virtual pets? They're still around, and girls like the virtual screen pets as well. When members of the public library teen advisory group in Worthington, Ohio, were asked to list their favorite tech gadgets, girls mentioned cell phones, iPod/MP3 players, digital cameras, flash drives, television, TiVo, and DVD players (Pechacek, 2007).

On the other hand, teenage girls still see computers as male territory and feel more computer anxiety than males do. These fears arise from stubborn gender stereotypes and gendered attribution theory in which females downplay their own ability and males overestimate their prowess. As a result, teenage girls continue to enjoy computers less than boys and perform less well with them (Cooper & Weaver, 2003).

What is the picture in schools? Probably, if for no other reason than administrative, technology such as school record-keeping and telecommunications remains computer-based. Computer labs remain a common means for incorporating technology into learning. Portable devices are not front and center for most school administrators, in much the same way that many computer applications do not resonate with teenage girls. However, showing how technology impacts the entire school endeavor would be a useful activity for girls, making them more aware of technology's educational role. Likewise, understanding how portable devices can impact learning would benefit cautious administrators.

When asked what technology they thought would be good for the classroom, students listed a number of products:

- Laptop computers to access digital textbooks and to process learning
- Cell phones to collaborate and capture images, as well as a new Mobile Prep service that permits users to create and study flashcards
- Digital cameras to capture images, including what is written on the classroom whiteboard
- Video cameras to tape classes and analyze one's own performance
- Web cams to talk with experts or other educational communities
- iPods to store data
- Graphing calculators to manipulate data
- Nintendo DS to play mind games ("Sky's the Limit," 2007)

SOFTWARE

Hardware may be the technology hook for boys, but *doing* something is a greater hook for girls. Unlike boys, who like software mainly for its entertainment value, girls want to learn something and apply their learning (Lepper & Malone, 1987). How can technology help them build relationships, have fun, or save the world? In professional and educational worlds, technology decisions tend to start by identifying the issue or task, then determining effective software, and only then choosing the hardware. So girls are modeling effective real-world behaviors.

When companies started to target software to teenage girls, they tended to fall back onto stereotypical themes: fashion, hairdos, horses. Small independent companies such as Purple Moon, founded by a mother who wanted to help her daughter enjoy technology, tried to produce more girl-empowered software but found it difficult to survive in the larger market. To this day, most software is written by males, which accounts for some of the hesitancy shown by girls (Lynn, Raphael, Olefsky, & Bachen, 2003).

How do teenage girls view software? Girls have made their interests known: They eschew violent, closed-universe games. They enjoy adventure games, role-playing games, storytelling and narrative, and open-ended applications that are content neutral (e.g., authoring tools, concept mapping, web design). They also like to use software to communicate and create (Van Eck & the AIM Lab at the University of Memphis, 2006). In terms of software design elements, girls want graphics, reality-based visuals and audio, interactive communication, complex but not frustrating activities, and images that portray a variety of girls (Fiore, 1999).

If the focus in choosing software is to optimize its benefits for girls now and in the future, then software that can help in school as well as at home makes the most sense. When the Centre for Learning & Performance Technologies (2007) asked more than 100 leading learning professionals from around the world (predominantly representing North America) to list the top technology learning software tools, the following products made the top 10 list for 2007:

1. Firefox web browser
2. del.icio.us social bookmarking tool
3. Skype VOIP (voiceover internet protocol) and instant messaging tools
4. Google search engine
5. GMail web-based e-mail
6. WordPress blogging tool

7. Google Reader RSS/Feed reader
8. PowerPoint presentation tool
9. Blogger
10. Word

Note the trends. All are free software except PowerPoint and Word (and OpenOffice is a free Open Source competitor to Microsoft's Office Suite). All the tools are web-based except PowerPoint and Word. The majority focuses on telecommunications and social networking. Most enable the user to create content. In short, these technology tools meet girls' desires for social learning. With so many schools so concerned about security that they ban telecommunications, perhaps the underlying message is that learning in school benefits from learning outside school. Families and community members, therefore, play an increasingly important role in supporting girls' learning, particularly in terms of using technology purposefully, by providing computer systems and Internet connectivity.

DIGITAL DOCUMENTS

While software long constituted the mainstay content for computers, other types of digital documents have emerged, thanks to the ever-growing number of digital storage devices such as MP3 and DVD players. Teenagers have bought records and tapes for decades. The newer formats, starting with CDs, are more flexible because of their random-access points, enabling users to locate their favorite selections instantly. More than ever, teens enjoy listening to spoken words and music, as well as viewing e-books and videos—sometimes simultaneously.

Because tastes in entertainment are significantly shaped by societal norms, gender-linked preferences exist. For instance, teens like music to evoke moods; when girls are lonely, they are likely to choose love music, which boys would eschew. Girls prefer classical and folk music, while boys prefer rock (Zillman & Gan, 1997). Likewise, boys tend to favor action movies, while girls prefer movies about relationships. These gender lines are most pronounced during the adolescent years (Fischoff, Antonio, & Lewis, 1998).

Even though these physical digital products remain on the market, they have been overshadowed by downloadable electronic versions. Now teens routinely search client-server sources such as iTunes and Rhapsody for music and eBooks and eReader for books. Downloading services may charge money per document accessed or charge a subscription fee; other document services provide public domain files for free, such as the Gutenberg Project and Partners in Rhyme. Teens also share digital files through peer-to-peer networking (e.g., Morpheus, Kazaa, Gnutella), which may well sidestep intellectual property laws. Another file dissemination product, BitTorrent, is described as an Open Source user group model.

The entertainment industry plays watchdog for pirated materials and is arresting middle schoolers as well as adults for copyright infringement. Therefore, teens need to know about media copyright laws as an ethical consideration as well as to avoid being arrested for criminal action. Girls are less likely to pirate digital documents, but they still need to be knowledgeable.

TELECOMMUNICATIONS

Telecommunications provide a natural hook for girls' technology engagement, particularly as these communication channels facilitate personal relationships and a sense of community. Females now constitute the majority of telecommunicators (U.S. Department of Commerce, 2004). Furthermore, 96% of 9- to 17-year-olds use social networking sites. While parents may despair of girl talk, a 2007 survey by the National School Boards Association found that nearly 60% of 9- to 17-year-olds talk about educational topics, from homework to college planning. Technology production and broadcasting, be it via blogs or podcasting, offer effective ways for girls to express themselves creatively.

Nothing replaces real-time communication. For this reason, telephones remain a top technology for teens, particularly for girls. Not surprisingly, e-mail constituted a popular Internet application until instant messaging (IM) surpassed it. Three-quarters of teenagers online use IM, and almost half of *all* teens IM *daily* (Lenhart, Madden, & Hitlin, 2005). With text-messaging capabilities, both large computers (i.e., desktops and laptops) and portable computers (e.g., cell phones and PDAs) can carry out that function. Indeed, as handheld devices become more sophisticated, such as iPhone and Oasis, function and device are merging as well. Unfortunately, schools are wary of such merged power and cramp the style of many teens by forbidding them to carry these pocket devices or engage in electronic conversation.

The World Wide Web, with its graphical interface, also transformed telecommunications, making it much more accessible for users. The Internet has lost much of its "geekiness," so that girls feel more comfortable using it than before. The transparent melding of text, sound, and image also helps users with different learning styles. As with other technologies, girls tend to use the Internet more for communication and learning, while boys see it as an entertainment channel (Kaiser Family Foundation, 2005).

Chapter 6

Girls' Access to Technology

While access to technology is necessary, it is not sufficient. Teenage girls need to know how to understand and use technology protocols and features efficiently and purposefully. They also need to understand the legal and ethical issues that technology poses. This chapter suggests ways for adults to help girls gain physical and intellectual access ethically.

PHYSICAL ACCESS

These days, most teenagers can find a computer to access, be it at a friend's house or in a public space. However, such access assumes a conscious effort that might not be a high priority for girls who do not see the importance of technology. Furthermore, those available systems might have little software and limited Internet connectivity. If users experience frustration in using technology, they are less likely to continue use.

For that reason, schools and libraries play a significant role in providing physical access because use is freely available, as opposed to Internet "parks" or other public kiosks. Nevertheless, public institutions might have insufficient numbers of systems to handle the demand or might provide outdated equipment with slow Internet connectivity. In addition, their operating hours might be inconvenient for night-owl teens. Because boys tend to be more physically aggressive, they might corner the computer "market." Because girls want to maintain positive human relationships, they are unlikely to confront such male behavior. For these reasons, adults in charge of technology access should consider means to ensure equity of access, such as the following:

- A couple of girls-only and boys-only computer systems
- Single-sex tech clubs (Dobosenski, 2001)
- Sign-up use sheets, which prompt students to plan ahead
- Free bus passes for younger teens to get to public-access sites more easily
- Longer access hours
- Circulating laptops
- A variety of computers to match needs (e.g., a lower-end system without Internet connectivity for word processing or other productivity applications versus a multimedia system for video editing)

INTELLECTUAL ACCESS

Getting girls' hands on technology is not sufficient. They must become comfortable and confident technology users. Youngsters tend to learn about technology by playing around with it themselves or by learning from their associates. Being greater risk-takers, boys are more likely than girls to explore technology, trying to "push the envelope." Public discussion of about the millennial generation has actually disadvantaged girls, since many adults assume that today's teenagers were born with a technology chip in their brains and that formal technology instruction is therefore unnecessary.

Just as reading and writing need to be taught explicitly, so, too, should technological operations be formally introduced. Adults also have to ensure that all youngsters have opportunities for practicing these technological skills. As students enter adolescence, they want meaningful and authentic tasks associated with technology. Girls, in particular, need a concrete reason to use technology. One good way to help teens gain technology skills focuses on a desired outcome, such as publicizing an event. To make attractive flyers, one needs to learn how to do desktop publishing. To publicize on the Internet, one needs to know how to create a web page. To create podcasts, one needs to learn how to record and edit audio. To produce a public service broadcast, one needs to learn how to record and edit video. In short, the content and the message drive the need to learn and practice technology skills.

Girls more than boys are likely to blame themselves if there's a technical problem—and attribute success to the machine rather than to their own abilities. Therefore, when girls get stumped, try to focus on the problem rather than the person ("So what did you want to accomplish? What happened—or didn't work? Let's figure out how to solve the problem."). Here are more tips for engaging teenage girls in learning about technology:

- Provide choice.
- Get the girls' input—and act on it.
- Incorporate social activity and collaborative learning. Encourage buddy learning and coaching.
- Emphasize communication and other forms of building relationships as a motive for incorporating technology.
- Offer low-risk activities, and encourage intellectual risk-taking by ensuring a safe learning environment: "It's OK to make mistakes."
- Emphasize effort more than mastery.
- Break down the instruction into manageable steps.
- Provide timely and specific feedback.
- Have a sense of humor—and encourage fun.

Several of these strategies apply to both sexes. Likewise, barriers to intellectual access are gender neutral: language issues, reading issues, lack of background knowledge, learning disabilities, physical disabilities, and so forth. Being able to identify which factors impede learning helps adults apply the appropriate intervention to help girls overcome those obstacles.

EMOTIONAL AND SOCIAL ACCESS

Just because girls *can* access technology does not mean that they *want* to access and use technology. Especially in their teenage years, girls are very aware of the social norms in their environment. If it is not considered cool by a social group to use technology, then girls in that clique probably will not touch computers—at least not openly. Furthermore, if they do like technology and use it surreptitiously, they may feel conflicted because they are keeping secrets from their friends (Center for Media Education, 2007; Eckes & Trautner, 2000).

Family behavior also impacts emotional and social access. For several reasons, parents are more likely to acquire a computer for sons than daughters. Parents hold outdated stereotypes about technology; more fathers than mothers used computers at an early age; male adults tend to use computers for a greater percent of the time than female adults; and parents think that computers help motivate their sons to do homework (Compaine, 2001; Jennings, 2000). As girls experience male-dominated technology at home, they may want to join in but not push for equal time, or they may reject technology in favor of activities that are perceived as more feminine and are more rewarded by parents, such as cooking or babysitting. Some cultures perpetuate these gender-specific roles, so those girls who want to pursue technological activities may be considered rebellious or disrespectful to their community.

While some technology applications are almost ubiquitous and gender neutral at this point, such as cell phones and digital players, others still have sex-linked connotations, such as video games and programming, which attract boys more than girls. Web 2.0, with its social networking opportunities, can be a natural fit for teenage girls. Several tools enable girls to talk with each other and contribute their own knowledge for the betterment of the group: online chats, blogs, wikis, document sharing, social bookmarking, and virtual realities. e-Groups offer an "insider" feeling. While being invited into an online group can make one feel special, the girl who is *not* invited can feel rejected, so adults should monitor these kinds of sites or frontload them so that *all* girls are invited. On the other hand, the online aspect of these sites offers a safer social distance for girl who are less outgoing or who have experienced social rejection.

Multimedia production and broadcasting also seem to be positive experiences for most girls, particularly if the end product is the result of collaboration. Thus, web page design and video productions offer good venues for girls to express themselves using technology. As girls gain more expertise, they may find that they are learning advanced technology skills such as coding and electronics, which can lead to programming and engineering careers.

When digital products are created in order to help others, such as creating a website for an animal rights group or producing a public service announcement, girls are more likely to be motivated to participate because a concrete reason exists for the activity.

Sometimes it makes sense to start with the service angle and then show how technology can be used to facilitate social change.

ETHICAL ACCESS

Some millennials show marvelous technological ability. Many can thumb-type at remarkable speed, learn new equipment intuitively, and multitask among technologies. Nevertheless, the ethical part of the human brain is the last section of the brain to develop. Just because many teens can do things with technology does not mean that they *should* do some things with technology. Although hacking reflects the teenage need for experimentation and risk-taking, it is illegal. On the positive side, teenage girls are less likely to take risks with technology, but at the same time they need encouragement to explore the possibilities of technology—as long as it is safe and legal.

Girls are more likely than boys to obey the rules and follow directions, but they still need to know those regulations. The issue of plagiarism needs to be addressed. Girls are most likely to run afoul of the law when they put copyrighted materials on their websites, such as song lyrics or Disney characters. Therefore, librarians and other adults need to alert all teenagers about intellectual property. For girls, citing the issue of fairness is usually enough to do the trick; girls can empathize with individuals who work hard to develop a unique logo, for instance, only to have another person rip it off for personal gain.

Additionally, teens risk endangerment when they put their own or their friends' pictures on Facebook or other social networking sites. With their interest in socializing and belonging, teenage girls might well put themselves in vulnerable situations that pedophiles and other sexual predators will take advantage of. Fortunately, today's teenagers are becoming savvier about predatory Internet lurkers, transferring the message of not talking to strangers to a cyberspace environment. Most youth realize that they shouldn't post their home address or Social Security number, but some teens forget how easy it is to locate a person given a school name or other information. A quick reminder to girls in particular is a good idea. Librarians can remind them that even fake identities can be traced by experienced tech users, and websites that were created and accessed only once can endure for years to embarrass the naive girl (Johnson, 2003).

Ethical issues also have to be addressed in terms of "consuming" online information. Teens, particularly girls, can be surprisingly trusting about information garnered from the Internet. They tend to believe and trust in information sources. In its report about search engine users (Fallows, 2005), the Pew Internet and American Life Project founded that almost two-thirds of users were not aware of sponsored sites (Horringan, 2007). Sirsi vice president Stephen Abram (2007) mentions several aspects of possible unethical practices by media developers. Here are three major areas of concern:

- *Advertising.* The main purpose of advertising is to inform— and to persuade. Advertising messages can be compelling, seducing young people into buying or agreeing with the advertising message without fully thinking about the consequences. Movies can embed advertising messages, and the Internet features sponsored sites and banners to attract users; in addition, websites can activate cookies in order to track user search habits. Search engine optimization is a surreptitious approach to getting a company's name displayed prominently. Companies can pay search engine providers to rank their websites on the first search-result page, where people are more likely to click on them. Librarians need to help teens examine the message, the company's agenda, and the means of communicating so young people can make informed decisions about advertisements. In addition, they need to explain how the Internet captures online behavior to target marketing efforts. Students also need to know how to turn off a cookie and other tracking features on the Internet in order to optimize privacy.
- *Wikis.* These socially constructed web pages are the result of numerous people's contributions, which can include mass media insiders. For example, several movies have been watched because of the online word-of-mouth instigated by mass media insiders. Librarians should explain how wikis

are produced and help students identify the contributors' credentials in order to ascertain the veracity of their content.

• *Sign-ups.* Increasingly, access to websites requires online registration. Often the site entices the reader, stating that the information will be free and that the registration is a simple one-time task that activates a log-in and password protection for the user. However, whatever information is provided by the user should be considered as accessible by the public, particularly since many enterprises sell the database created from the registration information. Students need to check the site carefully to discern what permissions and privacy rights are considered.

Not only commercial entities but also unscrupulous organizations and individuals can manipulate teenagers and exploit their tendencies to experiment and explore. Nevertheless, social networking provides opportunities for teenagers to develop social skills and collaborate. Since social networking is increasingly popular with most teenagers, especially girls, adults need to seriously consider its role in educational and youth-serving settings. For example, schools might consider providing intranet-based social networking experiences in order to help students learn how to negotiate ethical, safe interpersonal communication and collaboration. Librarians and other educators also need to teach teenagers how to identify safe social networking environments, such as Whyville.net and Imbee.com. Typically, these sites require that youth pass some kind of qualifying test and that parents be involved; often, these sites mention approvals by youth-serving organizations. OnGuardOnline, established by the Federal Trade Commission, has developed an kid-friendly interactive online quiz titled Buddy Builder (www.onguardonline.gov/quiz/socialnetworking_quiz.html) about safe and ethical social networking practices. In the final analysis, teaching teenage girls how to protect themselves and act ethically is a more effective and empowering approach than trying to protect them from inevitable unethical encounters.

Chapter 7

How Girls Can Use Technology

Probably the easiest way to get teenage girls engaged in technology is to build on their existing success as grand communicators (Agosto, 2004; American Association of University Women, 2000). While it is important for girls to be informed consumers of information, they should also be encouraged to become active creators of digital information (Hobbs, 2007; Keeble & Loader, 2001). Furthermore, because teenage girls can be very idealistic, getting involved in causes that are important to them, showing how technology can change society for the good can be very compelling. Above all, adults should help teenage girls reframe technology use from a source of immediate personal gratification to an empowering tool for self-fulfillment and social change (Children's Partnership, 2000; Katz, Rice, & Aspden, 2001). This chapter provides examples of ways to help girls gain critical skill in assessing, using, manipulating, and sharing ideas for immediate fun and for lifelong benefit.

THE GRAND COMMUNICATORS

The tipping point for girls using the Internet was telecommunications; when they saw the computer as a way to talk with others, girls were willing to get on the bandwagon. Now the majority of telecommunicators is female, reflecting girls' interest in relating to others and sharing experiences.

Of course, standard desktop computers are not required for digital communication; cell phones, particularly those with text messaging, enable girls to chat happily for hours. Nor can one assume that girls who can IM fluently are technologically competent. Furthermore, many school sites prohibit cell phones and e-mailing, so these natural tendencies are cut off even before their possible positive learning effect is considered.

Because digitally based communication is one component of technological competence, adults can use girls' communication ability as a natural starting point for facilitating technological skill. Because technology breaks down barriers of time and space, its use can appeal to girls who want a natural and continuous flow of communication. Moreover, conversations can cross classrooms, sites, and countries. What do girls around the globe think about global warming? How are family dynamics defined culturally? Telecommunication can be fun as an end itself, but it becomes more powerful when it can be used purposefully to help solve personal problems, assist with homework, and make a positive difference in the world.

Additionally, unlike traditional telephones, digital technology can also transmit images, providing a richer exchange. Therefore, whenever possible, adults should incorporate technology that facilities immediate and multimodel interaction. In the process, girls can learn how to capture, digitize, and embed information in a variety of formats. Adults should also help teens learn how to discern which format is most effective to communicate each message to each audience.

Here are some easy first steps in using telecommunications with youth, taking advantage of girls' interests and ways of knowing:

- Create an intranet that permits a safe telecommunication "universe" within the institution, be it in school or within a youth agency. Program-specific online "accounts" can authenticate users and monitor efforts. Girls can feel safer and freer to take calculated risks.
- Use threaded discussions, which can also be conducted within an intranet, to track individuals' perspectives on a topic. Teachers can use threaded discussion as a way to diagnose prior learning as well as analyze learning along the way. To optimize students' comments, authentic and open-ended questions should be posed, and timely, personalized feedback should be provided. Enabling teens to post their own questions or topics fosters engagement and empowerment. Threaded discussion can even be used

as a form of study-group help. Other youth-serving agencies can also use threaded discussion as an opportunity for girls to share their thoughts about personal areas of interest, from tips for babysitting to support during a divorce in the family. Adults should probably monitor these contributions, although most young people have become savvy about appropriate online chat and know how to apply peer pressure to minimize off-kilter comments; a team of peer reviewers can offer an opportunity for girls to assume responsibility and gain leadership skills. If a threaded discussion feature is not available, groups can use e-mail as an ersatz threaded discussion through the use of the reply feature (making sure that the e-mail service is set up to copy the prior message in the reply). In either case, these online discussions are particularly beneficial because the conversations are archived.

- Use e-mail and online chat to create collaborative documents such as reports and presentations. The Tracking feature of Microsoft Word enables each person to use a different color to change content or make comments. Teachers can use this feature to determine the quality of each person's contributions to the final product. Some real-time online chat programs include a common "whiteboard" that enables everyone to look at the same document simultaneously and mark on it.
- Use Internet meeting software to hold conversations in real time. Skype is particularly appealing because it permits one to make international telephone calls for free. Both microphone and webcam features may be used, which makes the experience more authentic. While speakerphones provide real-time interaction with parties on the other side of the line, seeing the other person adds another dimension of reality. If camcorders or digital document presenters are attached to the computer system, then participants can share images of their immediate environment, which provides a contextualized experience: "You are there, thanks to cyberspace." This kind of interactive cybermeeting may be considered an "out-of-body" experience. To optimize those experiences, adults should help youth prepare ahead of time, developing a set

of questions, practicing interviewing techniques, using the equipment, and projecting one's voice audibly.

- Use wikis to build community-based knowledge. No html experience is needed, but youth can benefit from online web page development and broadcasting options. Another useful feature of wikis is that each submitted version is saved, so the participants can see the changes over time. Individuals can either change the content or make comments to the content. Protocols can be established from the start, or participants can create protocols based on their experiences as they progress; this latter approach is more engaging and encourages intellectual risk-taking for girls. To ensure safety and confidentiality, it is a good idea to make the wiki a private space that is password protected.
- Include interactive features in educational and agency websites, such as interactive polls and comment "boxes." Youth really enjoy inputting their views and getting instant information about others' perspectives (for example, ranking favorite movies). While national or commercial polls are fun to do, creating local or site-specific polls can be more useful, such as best places to study after 9 P.M. or good sites for volunteer opportunities. Even better, have girls create their own polls or online questions. As with other teen-developed content, adults can monitor communication or they can delegate such responsibility to teens, making sure that expectations are clear from the start and stating upfront that adults have access to anything that teens might input.

GIRLS JUST WANT TO HAVE FUN

As Mary Poppins said, "In every task to be done there's an element of fun." Making technology a serious course of study or a means of high-stakes testing situation is a sure way to disengage girls. Because teenage girls have to deal with daily challenges and often react in a stressed fashion, lowering the stress factor relative to technology is vital. To that end, the technology should be easy to learn and as transparent as possible; that is, the focus should be on the content and experience, not the technology. Second, the content and situation should also be low stress; the possibility of failure should be minimal. By experiencing technology in a fun way, girls gain skill while focusing on the content. In the process, they can discover that technology can be useful as well.

So what's fun for girls? Ask them! While some activities are fun for both boys and girls, many technology games do not interest girls, such as violent, shoot-'em-up games or games that consist of a closed universe of task-based levels. Instead, girls prefer open-ended adventure games, applications that enable them to express themselves, and communication-based technology.

Because the word on the street is more likely to point to the usual list of commercial and Web 2.0 sites, adults should actively help girls locate appropriate fun through interactive, appealing websites and software, ideally ones that are targeted to teenage girls. Increasingly, these sites include features that draw in girls and make them feel more involved. For instance, girls might get to dress up a character or solve a puzzle; instant polls and comment areas allow girls to voice their opinions and get feedback.

Adults should also enlist the help of teenage girls in reviewing and recommending such websites. When those URLs are connected to a school or youth-serving agency portal or wiki, they signal to girls that adults can have fun, too, and recognize that girls want to have fun and relax. Here is a sampling of fun websites:

- www.uah.edu/colleges/liberal/womensstudies/girls. html—a metasite of links recommended by a 14-year-old girl
- www.links4kids.co.uk/girlsonly.htm—another metasite that includes educational links
- www.girlscouts.org
- www.zoeysroom.com
- www.gurl.com
- www.zwinky.com
- www.mypopstudio.com

Several public libraries list fun sites on their web portal. Here is a sampling:

- Haverhill (Massachusetts) Public Library: teencybercenter. org

- Hennepin County (Minnesota) Public Library: www.hclib.
  org/teens/
- Skokie (Illinois) Public Library: www.skokie.lib.il.us/s_
  teens/tn_links/
- Weld (Colorado) Public Library: www.mylibrary.us/
- Library media specialist Cathy Rettberg (2006) sponsors an
  online book discussion group and has gathered a number
  of book club URLs targeted to teens: www.bookdivas.com,
  community.livejournal.com/notyourmothers, teenreads.
  com, and www.washingtonreads.org/blog

To be sure, technology is not confined to the Internet; it can anything with a plug or a battery (including hair dryers). Even in the arena of digital technology, there are lots of fun tech tools: scanners, cameras and camcorders, gaming equipment, and so on. Here are a few ways that youth-serving agencies and other stakeholders can support tech fun for girls:

- Increasingly, libraries and other recreational centers are
  holding gaming events that include activities such as Dance
  Dance Revolution, Guitar Hero, Wii Sports, and karaoke.
  Girls can also bring their favorite video games to play
  cooperatively. These centers should consider having a Girls
  Night Out event so that girls can have fun without having
  the pressure of dealing with the male species.
- Movie night is a mainstay community event, particularly in
  the summer, when outdoor screens can be put up in public
  park areas. Movies made by teenage girls can enrich the
  offerings and give youth a public venue to showcase their
  creativity.
- Online mother–daughter book clubs are a fun, easy
  way for females to connect locally and globally (e.g.,
  byforandaboutwomen.com/motherdaughterclub.html).

I AM A MATERIAL GIRL

One approach to involving girls in technology is consumer oriented. That is, girls select and "consume" information. Girls might search websites that feature fashion, entertainment, personal advice, and so on. In some cases, girls may want to buy a product or service; in other cases, they merely want to see what is out there or access information that they can use. Japanese teenage girls are the embodiment of consumer technology, wearing the latest techie gadgets and communicating with multimodal cell phones. For many of them, technology is a lifestyle choice; tech accessories such as cases and dangly cell phone "strings" crowd the marketplace. In fact, the Japanese cell phone business is so advanced that the government has not made a substantial effort to wire the country; the population is wifi-centric. In the United States, technology can be bought on the street and accessed from public sites.

Using gadgets as a focus of consumer technology, girls can practice savvy consumerism by comparing features, prices, and service options of desired technology such as cell phones, digital players, and cameras. They can create girl-centric wikis about these and other products, giving each other advice based on their research and experience. Girls can learn more about using the products by downloading manuals (e.g., www.retrevo.com), reading online tutorials (e.g., www.kidzonline.com/TechTraining/), listening to podcasts, watching videocasts, and participating in teen workshops. Girls can also become tech tool experts, creating their own training products.

Realizing the power of teen girls' pocketbooks, especially in terms of disposable income, marketers have targeted this population heavily. Girls might be surprised at the attention given to them by big business. eMarketer researched the teen marketing scene and successfully sold its 2005 marketing report *Kids and Teens: Blurring the Line Between Online and Offline* for $695. To help make teens more aware of marketing strategies, the Media Awareness Network (2007) created a student worksheet, noting a variety of images that advertisers use to entice the teenage market: ideal teens, families having fun, excitement, popular celebrities, cartoon figures, sex appeal; other tactics include using compelling personal stories, playing memorable sounds and songs, giving misleading facts and omitting important ones, promising popularity, and repeating messages endlessly so that they are imprinted in teens' brains. MarketResearch.com maintains a lengthy bibliography of market research about the teen market (www.marketresearch.com/map/

cat/1446.html). Here is a sampling of companies that focus on the youth market:

- www.KidClubMarketing.com
- www.fusemarketing.com
- www.alloymarketing.com/media/tweens
- www.collegiatepromotions.com
- www.campusmediagroup.com

Because advertising can be very enticing, teenage girls need to monitor their online spending habits. Just as important, teens need to be reminded about the possible dangers of providing credit card and other personal information online.

As another promotional strategy, teens are now being targeted as marketers themselves. Increasingly, companies and marketers spot trendsetting teens and hire them as popular culture consultants and communicators. For example, booksellers are focusing on teens by using MySpace, providing interactive teen-centric cyberspaces to talk about authors and books, sponsoring teen writing contests, creating online blog tours, producing online exclusive interviews, and giving teens advance copies of books so they can broadcast their early reviews to peers (Sellers, 2007). Another new spin-off from MySpace is MySpace Fashion, which looks at the latest trends, often featuring and generated by teens. While it might be said that teenagers are being manipulated as they give first-hand information that will profit businesses, teenage girls can take advantage of these opportunities to truly speak their mind and influence corporations. If girls want more inclusive images and more girl-empowering messages, then communicating with marketers can advance their cause.

I AM WOMAN, HEAR ME ROAR

Girls also like to take advantage of Web 2.0. On the consumer end, girls can go to Flickr and YouTube to find fun images and multimedia that other peers have posted. Girls will often e-mail their friends about fun files. More important, though, girls become motivated to create and share their own content. Blogs enable girls to read and post electronic diaries, and many such applications allow readers to post comments. Wikis provide a group-created knowledge base. Facebook and MySpace are extremely popular sites for sharing one's personal life—or persona—with peers. The opportunities to belong to these online communities and contribute at one's own comfort level can be very enticing for teenage girls.

On the other hand, these cyberspaces are usually open to everyone, including unscrupulous adults. Increasingly, teens have gotten savvy about this potential danger, absorbing the 21st-century version of "don't talk to strangers." Unfortunately, they sometimes forget the lasting consequences of words and images shared online; even when they think they have erased an inappropriate entry, teens may find that someone along the way has saved that file, and will later incriminate them. Girls may be especially vulnerable to this situation since a party-happy picture may encourage males to follow up with action even years later—or may turn off a prospective employer.

Youth-serving institutions should also have production areas and technology tools so girls can *produce and disseminate* their own original content for fun. The tools might be as basic as word-processing programs, which allow girls to do creative writing and journaling, and instruction in how to do word art, import images, and add sounds, all of which make girls' writing more fun and media-rich. Webcams and cameras enable girls to capture personally interesting images, and editing software can make those images look more professional. Girls may also need help learning how to transfer files (Chandler-Olcott & Mahar, 2001, 2003).

Local communications companies can also invite teenage girls to do production work or create content. Teens can be interviewed on local radio stations; a girls-only talk show can give teenagers a voice. Local public-access cable television channels can feature teenage girls as talent, as commentators, as community activists, or as positive models for children. These TV franchises can also train teenage girls to create shows: as camera crew, audio experts, editors, directors, and producers. School- or community-based youth groups can even create weekly or monthly shows about teen life.

While it might be motivating to have some cute boy show girls how to do such technology tasks, it would probably be more empowering to have females, both teen and adult, show tech novices the ropes. College-age girls and young female professionals are key players in this tech mentoring; they are young enough to remember their teenage years and can connect emotionally to younger girls at the same time that they provide a compelling model for future technology use.

THE TIMES THEY ARE A-CHANGIN'

Girls want to make a difference. They can become passionate about causes, be it global warming or saving animals at the local shelter. Technology can help them locate information and research issues, organize and communicate their thoughts, and actually solve problems. Technology also expands their impact because it can connect like-minded teenage girls and mentors around the world so they can collectively address various issues.

The nonprofit organization Mind on the Media has a project titled "Turn Beauty Inside Out," which tries to instill independent thinking and critical analysis of media messages. To this end, the project actively enlists the input and participation of teenage girls. Each year it focuses on a unique theme and concludes with a conference that brings together girls and adults (mainly women). Its 2004 campaign focused on media images of women in politics. At a conference in Washington, D.C., about 50 girls gained leadership skills as they interacted with women political leaders. Together, the females developed a set of recommendations, including picturing women in power positions, showing a wide variety of women, covering women politicians in men's magazines, and focusing on women's accomplishments more than their body images.

Here is a sampling of other teen-centric technology initiatives that focus on social issues:

- Technology for Social Change (www.tecsChange.org) provides technology resources and training for grassroots groups around the world. Its YouthTech program includes speakers and forums on social change using technology.
- The University of Michigan's Institute for Research on Women and Gender sponsors the program GEMS: Girls Explore Mathematics through Social Science (www.umich.

edu/~irwg/research/current/gems.html). It focuses on middle school girls, building on students' interest in social issues. Both workshops and online tutorials give girls tools to gather and analyze data (see its website: www.smartgirl. org).
- MIT's Learn 2 Teach, Teach 2 Learn Program teaches teenagers engineering concepts as well as graphic and web design. Students then go into the community and teach peers what they had learned. They also work to help solve community problems by using technology (Hoffmann, 2007).
- McDonald's Teens for the Cure® program incorporates science education as it involves teens in projects to address breast cancer.

I LOVE YA TOMORROW!

Sometimes it may seem that girls just live only in the "now," but many are contemplating—and fearing—the future. One problem confronting them is the lack of enough accurate and current information to make informed decisions. Several services can help girls get the information they need:

- College and career counselors need to update their knowledge about technology and other knowledge-based careers. They should map out the courses needed to apply to colleges in the majors desired by targeted companies and make sure that girls know their options in plenty of time to plan ahead. These counselors can also create web pages linking to college and career-planning URLs, noting the impact of technology. A girls-only page can provide targeted information so girls will not decline to access such information.
- Libraries should include college and career information as well in a variety of formats. Librarians can hold workshops about technology futures and invite women professionals who use technology in their work. Librarians should also model their own technology skill and positive attitude, as well as encourage girls to help in the library with

technological services such as evaluating websites, coaching peers on technology, and creating technology-based products (e.g., flyers, newsletters, web pages, videos, podcasts).
- Schools and other youth-serving agencies can establish girls-only clubs that incorporate lifelong technology skills, such as photography, video, graphic design, animation, web design, marine biology, veterinary science, forensics, health and fitness, and so on.
- Girls can shadow women in industry or interview them, capturing the experience on audio or videotape. Girls can then edit the tapes to be broadcast or archived in libraries. Career women can mentor girls via telecommunications.

Increasingly, companies and organizations are creating websites about women in technology fields. Adults and girls can explore these sites to find out what kind of preparation they need to pursue those careers. Here is a starting list:

- www.witi.org
- www.womenintechnology.org
- www.womenintech.com
- www.gsdl.org
- www.expandingyourhorizons.org
- eamusic.dartmouth.edu/~wowem/
- www.ncwit.org/cisco
- quest.nasa.gov/women/intro.html

PART III

TECHNOLOGY-ENHANCED LEARNING ACTIVITIES

Chapter 8

In-School Incorporation

Schools serve as natural settings for engaging technology-based learning. Even with the U.S. Department of Education's National Education Technology Plan, the school community needs to pro-actively develop a coordinated curriculum and relevant learning activities that facilitate female involvement. The school library and its staff often spearhead technology initiatives and provide technology-rich resources, so they should collaborate actively with the rest of the school community through curricular-based technology planning and implementation (Agosto, 2004; Crew, 1997; O'Dell, 2002). Co-curricular offerings should also be considered. A variety of learning activities can be developed by teacher-librarians in collaboration with classroom teachers to reflect a variety of teenage girls' interests and career opportunities.

CONDITIONS FOR LEARNING

Technology is driving large-scale social changes, affording unprecedented educational opportunities and radically changing the world of work for this generation of girls. Social responsibility and leadership are thus particularly important when considering the role of technology in education. The school community can now access resources from around the world, exchange perspectives with peers in other countries, obtain recent research on virtually any topic, view images from Mars and beyond, and run simulations of processes impossible to replicate in the classroom. With the incorporation of technology, educators and learners increase the repertoire of tools for analyzing, synthesizing, and sharing information. Ninety-nine percent of all public schools and more than 90% of U.S. classrooms are connected to the World Wide Web, and the ratio of instructional computers to students continues to increase (National Center for Education Statistics, 2003). Seventy-five percent of California students use technology in the classroom at least once a month (California State Department of Education, 2006). As a result of such trends, notions of what it means to be educated, or even literate, are also changing.

While technology has the demonstrated potential to be a socially positive force, it also can have negative consequences. For example, despite some progress toward promoting more equitable access to technology, a "digital divide" (Holloway, 2000) separates those who have access to technology and those who do not. While the difference in computer/student ratio of the richest and poorest schools is insignificant (California State Department of Education, 2006), the equity issues are far deeper than simple physical access to technologies. Students have a great deal to gain (or lose) from the manner in which information technologies are used. Students from poorer schools are less likely to use computers at school, particularly Hispanic students, African American students, and students with disabilities. These are the students who also are less likely to have access to computers at home (Patrick, 2004). On a positive note, while student use may differ, schools do provide the technology safety net for students of color and students in lower socioeconomic environments."At this point in time, the problem is not necessarily lack of funds, but lack of adequate training and lack of understanding of how computers can be used to enrich the learning experience"(U.S. Department of Education, 2004).

Despite technology's impact on education, research has shown that even tech-savvy teachers have difficulty incorporating technology into learning activities. Teachers feel that students do not have enough time on the computer but that they themselves need extra time to plan for computer activities (Bauer & Kenton, 2005). Furthermore, women more than men are likely to feel uncomfortable with technology, an attitude that is picked up by girls (Harris, 1999; Nicholson, Hancock, & Dahlberg, 2007). Therefore, the school community needs to ensure that teachers and other school personnel have regular opportunities to learn and apply skills for integrating computer technologies effectively. Furthermore, educational administrators must be at least as knowledgeable about the promise and pitfalls of these technologies as the teachers they will lead—if not more so. A program of ongoing faculty development and technology planning is essential if society wants to realize the potential of new learning technologies, especially for girls (U.S. Department of Education, 2004). More specifically, part of that training needs to address gender issues so that educators can ensure equitable access to technology.

PreK–12 schools constitute the official educational framework for formal learning in the United States. Particularly with the federal No Child Left Behind Act, PreK–12 education has a mandate to provide formal curricula and effective instruction that prepare today's young people to become productive, contributing citizens. Furthermore, the U.S. Department of Education's National Education Technology Plan (2004) stipulates that the school community should develop engaging technology-based learning. State and local governments have established regulations to ensure an equitable and accountable educational structure. In the final analysis, though, it is the district and school-site communities that make the final decisions that support the conditions for a community-relevant, coordinated curriculum and relevant learning activities that facilitate female engagement and competence. The Consortium for School Networking (2006) asserts that "visionary leadership and community and parental support seem to drive change in the most technology-intensive schools" (p. 2).

The North Central Regional Educational Laboratory (2004a) also identified community-committed vision as a necessary element for effective teaching and learning with technology. Other elements mentioned include teacher proficiency, access to resources and learning opportunities, schoolwide equity, alignment of school culture and research-based practice, and systematic thinking about the entire school endeavor.

In addressing equity issues, conditions for learning technology must consider girls' processing styles and cultural context (Cole & Griffin, 1987; DeVillar & Faltis, 1991). The following practices promote gender-affirming education:

- Broad-based vision and mission
- Positive and open community-based school culture
- Comprehensive, cohesive, and interdependent curriculum
- Competent and committed staff with a low student/teacher ratio
- A strong repertoire of instructional and learning strategies to address individual students' needs

• Systemic, aligned assessment that provides for alternative ways to measure student performance
• A rich collection of learning materials and fully integrated technology
• Well-maintained and spacious facilities that support the school vision (Farmer, 1996)

CURRICULUM

Adults must be mindful that technology alone will change very little in educational settings (Becker, 2003). Warschauer (2003) proposed a technology framework for social inclusion, with a focus on transformation rather than technology; this approach also addresses girls' need for relation-based experiences. In its 2003 report about information technology in education relative to girls, UNICEF made several recommendations:

• Use information and communication technology as a means to an end, not an end in itself.
• Use the Internet to collect information and collaborate.
• Use the Internet to foster an interactive learning environment.
• Promote cross-site communication via the Internet.

In short, education that integrates technology with sound pedagogies and that fosters girls' critical views of technology is vital.

In 2007 the International Society for Technology in Education revised its national educational technology standards for students, with the aim of identifying "what students should know and be able to do to learn effectively and live productively in an increasingly digital world" (p. 1). Building on a knowledge base of technical concepts and operations, students should know how to research, problem-solve, communicate, and collaborate effectively and responsibly using technology. The revised standards include a new emphasis on creativity and innovation, which can engage girls who might otherwise consider technology to be a dry, rote endeavor.

Because technology embraces social networking, digital

citizenship has gained central attention. Almost half of K–12 students do not consider hacking to be a crime. Internet plagiarism is increasing, cyberbullying is rampant, and cybercrime occurs without thinking (Baum, 2005). Therefore, technology-enhanced education must address digital rights and responsibilities such as intellectual property, netiquette, privacy, and security. The school community has to help students construct a moral compass by which to use technology responsibly. This curriculum element is particularly important for girls because they remain the more vulnerable sex in terms of online predators.

Technology is most effective when integrated as one component into learning environments and used as a tool for active construction and demonstration of higher levels of critical, creative thinking and problem solving (Brooks, 1993; Heinich, 1996; Papert, 1980). While technology can be a stand-alone curriculum (e.g., web design, programming), for *all* students to learn and apply technology, all educators should provide students with opportunities to learn and use technological tools within existing curricula.

INSTRUCTIONAL DESIGN

Staff need to be trained not only to use technology resources and tools but also to teach with them. They need to design instruction and help students learn how to use technology purposefully. Each step in creating technology-enhanced learning activities can be examined in light of technology and girls' needs.

Outcomes

What should students be able to know and do? The curriculum typically determines the student's learning outcome, although the relevant educators need to select the specific outcome at any one period. Technology skills can constitute part of the outcome; since girls usually need to see a concrete reason for pursuing an outcome, the identified technology needs to be an integral component in order to meet the outcome. For instance, in order for students to demonstrate the ability to analyze water, they might need to be able to use a scientific probe instrument.

Indicators

How well students meet those outcomes requires an assessment; this measurement can incorporate technology. For example, if research is a component of the outcome, students can learn how to locate and evaluate information online. A multimedia presentation can facilitate demonstrating a content outcome. Nevertheless, students need to have several ways to demonstrate knowledge, just as they have different ways of learning. If students develop a repertoire of technological tools, then they should be able to call on those tools in assessing their acquired knowledge. The assessment instrument prompt, for instance, should be gender neutral or have an option that acknowledges girls' interests (e.g., telecommunications, technology collaboration tools).

Learners' Characteristics

The more educators know about their students, the more effectively they can help students learn. What are individuals' interests and talents? What technology have they experienced—and how did they feel about it? Most students learn technology informally by exploring on their own or with friends. Because teenage girls are less likely to have computers and are less likely to take intellectual risks than boys, extra effort is needed to leverage girls' typical learning habits. Using telecommunications and collaborative tools builds on girls' relational skills. Providing concrete examples that speak to girls' interests helps them see a reason for learning technology. Designing learning activities that encourage self-expression and creativity engages girls cognitively and emotionally.

Prerequisite Skills

It should be noted that a technology-based assessment assumes that the student knows how to use that technology, so it is important for educators to assess students' prior knowledge about the technology tool and to teach that tool if it is necessary in order to demonstrate content knowledge. If collaborative groups are used in the activity, at least one girl in the group needs to be comfortable enough with the technology to teach it to her peers. One alternative method to address equity issues is to determine content and technology needs; particularly in the language arts, boys are more likely to need content remediation and girls are more likely to need technology instruction, so training can be single sex, with the girls going to the library or computer lab for targeted instruction.

Instructional Format

What resources facilitate learning? While most schools still use textbooks, a variety of other sources should be considered, including technology-based ones. The teacher-librarian is well positioned to recommend materials that are relevant, developmentally appropriate, and in a format that engages students with different learning styles. The location of these resources is also key. For instance, can students access the Internet from their classes or do they need to go to the library or computer lab? Selection of content should also consider gender interests; physics examples, for instance, might include a variety of sports rather than just football. Instructional format also includes the method of facilitating learning; demonstrations, case studies, role-plays, and simulations all provide concrete experiences that speak to girls' ways of learning. Small-group work, including discussion (be it face-to-face or online), enables students to improve their social skills, so decisions about group arrangement for academic and social tasks need to be determined when designing the instruction. Timing and sequencing also impact instructional choices, since incorporating technology must be calculated into the time frame; if technology skills need to be learned, then additional time may be needed upfront, but the use of technology can also shorten learning activity time (e.g., revising writing). In any case, students need to know from the start how technology will be incorporated (e.g., locating articles, creating a spreadsheet, making a videocast) so that they can do their work with that factor in mind. For example, if the final project will be a podcast, students need to focus on textual and oral information rather than visual resources.

Context

How does the instructional design, including technological aspects, fit into the larger picture of education—and into the lives of students? Isolated activities seldom lead to internalized learning. From the start, educators need to draw on students' prior experiences and feelings in order to help them make personal connections; this approach works particularly well with girls. In addition, girls seldom see technology as part of their future; realizing that technological tools can open more career doors and more lifestyle options may motivate girls. The environment in which students learn also affects instructional design; for instance, home computer access depends on the family's economic status, and boys are more likely than girls to get access when a computer must be shared. Therefore, it might be necessary to devote some class time to computer use rather than requiring students to do all technology work outside of school hours.

COLLABORATION

The effective implementation of technology-enhanced education requires a schoolwide commitment of resources and action. The governing body allocates funding and makes policy decisions that impact the availability and use of technology. The teaching staff determines and delivers curricula. The school library staff provides technology-rich resources and often spearheads technology initiatives. Technical staff maintains network services and related hardware; some technical specialists also train staff.

By systematically communicating and collaborating, the school community can optimize curricular-based technology planning and implementation (Agosto, 2004; Crew, 1997; O'Dell, 2002). On an organizational level, several elements need to be in place:

- Common vision and goals
- Effective communication and respect for differences
- Sufficient resources
- System infrastructure and support
- Continuously relevant processes
- Ongoing assessment and adjustments based on findings (California Alliance of K–18 Partnerships, 2004)

On an individual level, each person has technological skills, both in terms of using technological tools and applying technology to different functions, such as instruction, administration, and research. Additionally, availability of technology is usually uneven or decentralized, so that different departments are likely to build specialized expertise (e.g., scanning, podcasting, video editing, web design, use of scientific probes). No one person knows everything about technology or has access to everything, so identifying and collaborating with experts are key. Moreover, technology can facilitate collaboration because not everyone has to be at the same place at the same time in order to plan and work together.

It should be noted that, when telecommunicating, information has to be accessible to all relevant stakeholders. Since people might use different operating system platforms, have varying computer configurations, and use various software applications, a common standard needs to be established. Typically, saving e-mail and documents in .pdf format works for group reading. However, if documents are to be developed collaboratively, then .rtf files may be needed. Additionally, as Open Source applications gain more stability, they offer a cost-effective means for all stakeholders to have the same software for easier interoperability.

Even with physical and intellectual joint access to technology, collaboration still requires work. Individuals have to trust and depend on each other. Common goals and shared understanding must precede collaborative efforts. Stakeholders have to negotiate power and share control. Collaboration might start with a simple one-period lesson, during which the teacher-librarian shows students how to use online magazine indexes in order to locate current articles on a social issue.

With the advent of technology, the traditional hierarchy of seniority is being replaced by a flatter organization based on expertise. A community of learners more accurately reflects best practice relative to technology planning and implementation; "insiders" support newcomers, and the group focuses on school improvement. This paradigm resonates with feminist thinking and provides positive role models for teenage girls. Ideally, girls should participate in this community so they can see how leadership can be distributed throughout the community and can gain more influence themselves.

CO-CURRICULAR OPPORTUNITIES

The incorporation of technology into the school needs to transcend academics. Especially because some students see courses as work and co-curricular activities as fun, technology in school needs to include a playful side. Co-curricular endeavors offer additional means to address a variety of teenage girls' interests and link to career opportunities. Co-curricular activities are usually not graded, so girls are more likely to step outside their comfort zone to explore new possibilities, and these activities typically build on socially constructed interest groups that reinforce girls' need for relationships.

Here is a sampling of technology-enhanced co-curricular activities that are likely to attract teenage girls:

- Serving as library tech aides
- Online book clubs and literature circles
- Video service club
- Video yearbook
- Student publication clubs: newspaper, literary magazine, yearbook
- Photo or movie club
- Fashion club, using virtual bodies (e.g., www.glamour.com), websites (e.g., www.smarter.com/smartervisualsearch/select.php and www.popgloss.com/), and software (e.g., fashioncad.net/fashdown.htm)
- Music and drama clubs, creating podcasts of materials in the public domain
- Language and culture clubs, creating pod- and videocasts
- Spirit club, creating podcast cheers and multimedia presentations for rallies
- Serving as special education aides, helping with assistive technology
- Future teachers club, providing online tutoring for younger children

Service learning is another outlet for teenage girls' interest in helping others. Traditionally, service learning involves working in the community and linking those experiences to education (Hull & Schultz, 2002). However, co-curricular activities often include service clubs, which have a similar purpose. Technology can be incorporated in several ways:

- Podcasting community oral histories
- Videotaping local landmarks
- Developing an interactive online map mash-up of the community
- Online mentoring
- Teaching technology to elders and youngsters
- Creating audiobooks for day-care centers and hospitals
- Creating web pages for not-for-profit organizations
- Creating an online database of local hotlines or places where teens can volunteer
- Creating multimedia presentations for local social action
- Recycling cell phones to the homeless or to troops in the armed forces

SAMPLE ACTIVITIES

A variety of learning activities can be developed by the school community. Teacher-librarians are especially well positioned to collaborate with classroom teachers and other school personnel to incorporate technology meaningfully for teenage girls. The following six topics were chosen because they are highly preferred career choices by teenage girls (O'Dell, 2002).

Writing

Following and Creating Directions

One of the ways to learn how to use technology is to follow directions. These directions can be communicated in several formats: textual steps, written steps augmented by diagrams, podcasts, video/vidcasts. Even if the final product is oral, the directions are usually written first before transforming the information into another format. One person can write directions, such as how to do a technological process. A peer can try to follow the directions, documenting her experience through a think-aloud (captured through direct observation, audiorecording, or videorecording) or digital journaling. By providing feedback about the directions, peers can help each other communicate effectively. Feedback might mention wording, sequencing, and use of visuals or audio. With technology, solutions can incorporate a number of options.

Continuous Story

One person starts a story, be it in written or audio format. The story can be transferred by e-mail or online blog/wiki. The second person adds to it, transmitting the continuing story digitally. The story continues throughout the class or within a small group of students. The final story is reported to the entire class.

Peer-Reviewed Writing

One student posts or e-mails her writing. If the document uses Microsoft Word, each person can use a different color to track her edits and comments. Wikis can incorporate comments such that the main page is not changed, and even changes to the main page are captured each time the user saves the document. In either case, the classroom teacher and teacher-librarian can identify which person is making the changes. Students can decide whether to accept the changes or not, making them feel in control of their writing. To add more depth to the analysis, the writer can justify the reason for her editing decisions (i.e., why she accepted—or rejected—a specific change). This activity helps students improve their analysis of textual content, editing skills, and critical self-analysis.

Writing Commentary

Student writing or other existing documents, including e-books, can be enhanced through adding comments. This strategy can be used in several ways. Students can personalize a document in the public domain (e.g., a Shakespeare sonnet) through online comments, inserted images and sounds, hyperlinks and pop-up dialog boxes, or even simple changes in the font and background. A class can individualize the same document or each person can choose a unique document to "enhance." Students can copy-and-paste a document into a text box, with a parallel second column text box dedicated to commentary and other metacognitive reflections. Student-originated work can also be personalized by a peer. It should be noted that the document under examination can be a visual.

Collaborative Writing

A group can work on a collaborative research report. For such a collaboration to work well, the scope should be extensive enough that it would be hard for one person to manage it well within the time frame (e.g., life in medieval Paris). Each person could also focus on a different type of resource (e.g., monographs, magazines, newspapers, encyclopedias, videos, podcasts). Controversial topics or issues that lend themselves to several perspectives are also good candidates for collaborative projects. A significant factor is the designation of roles or workload; students may need help in this process. Even though it is tempting to have girls serve as collaboration experts, they also are able to promote insider/outsider divisions, so giving them such supervisory responsibility may be a two-edged sword.

All the World's a Stage

Small groups can create a skit or dramatic piece, transforming written information from one style (e.g., expository, narrative, descriptive) to drama format. This process also works well with contemporary issues that students have experienced or read about. Each person can assume the role of one character, researching credible behaviors and speech patterns for that role (e.g., a politician, a young mother, a social worker). Negotiating how the characters would interact enables students to experience sociocultural issues viscerally. Learning how to write so that the dialogue carries the story strengthens active language. Schlitz's 2007 book *Good Masters! Sweet Ladies!* provides a good model. Technology can be incorporated as each group creates an audio broadcast of their drama; a podcast or audiotape helps students focus on the words rather than costuming, which introduces another dimension.

Art and Design

Do You See What I See?

Students can take photos of their surroundings (e.g., school, neighborhood, shopping mall, park); post them on Flickr, Google Picasa, or PhotoBucket; and tag them (that is, assign subject headings) for retrieval. Students can take pictures of their class, their school, their neighborhood, an event, an example of a social issue, examples of technology, or people using technology. They can also take photos of the same subject matter throughout the year or semester to analyze the differences over time. Students can compare perspectives about the same subject matter or see how different topics are treated based on their own photos and on photos they locate online. Likewise, they can compare tagging efforts to determine how individuals categorize information. As an extension activity, photos can be linked and captioned to online maps as a mash-up.

Clip Art

Students tend to use clip art when they want to insert an image into a digital document; it's easy and it's convenient. However, such habits can be imaginatively stultifying and perhaps gender limiting (Binns & Branch, 1995). To help students become aware of possible gender- or age-linked trends, adults can ask students to choose an academic or personal topic, such as "science" or "shopping," and see what clip art is used. In the process, they can also identify specific design elements, such as use of color and space, as well as technique (e.g., photographic, iconic, cartoon). As students learn about graphic design, they can create their own set of clip art. Their work can be collected to form a database or repository of student-developed clip art that can be posted on the school's website. LeLoup and Ponterio (2007) provide simple online directions for creating clip art (http://www.cortland.edu/flteach/mm-course/clipart2.html).

Museum Curators

Collecting memorabilia is a way to maintain relationships.

Students can build on this hobby to explore the career of a museum curator. They can start by researching the job on online museums and occupational websites (e.g., www.bls.gov/oco/ocos065. htm). Students can also engage in online chat, videoconferencing, and telephone or live interviews with museum curators. Based on their knowledge, students can then examine online museums (e.g., Museum of Online Museums: www.coudal.com/moom/ and Virtual Library Museums: vlmp.museophile.com/) in light of possible e-exhibitions that they can "install." Like a professional curator, students need to research the artifacts and construct a guide for their exhibitions. Jamie McKenzie provides directions on creating a virtual museum (fno.org/museum/oldies&goodies. html) that can exhibit each student's or group's effort. Another free software for analyzing and sharing visual information is Transana.

The Ideal School

Students spend about half of their lives in schools: typically half of their waking hours and half of the year. That's a long time to spend in a setting about whose appearance they have little choice— except to keep it clean. How might it look? How could school facilities be designed to optimize students' experiences? Students can use Google Sketch Up or other simple computer-aided design (CAD) programs to design the perfect school. Students can focus on the overall building (a tendency of boys) or a room interior (a tendency of girls); ideally, groups can meld both approaches. Of course, CAD programs can be used to create any ideal setting: from teen bedroom to shopping mall to community. In each case, artistic concepts of three-dimensional modeling are being introduced and explored. Particularly since girls tend to have more difficulty than boys with spatial relationships, this activity motivates them to be creative about a concrete experience. Students can also research engineering and architecture careers to see who constructs schools (usually males) and consider how female designers might approach the task differently.

What Color Are You?

Color affects people's emotions and sense of well-being. Students can begin by researching websites that describe how color affects mood (e.g., www.colorgenics.com, brightworld.com/ Cool/Mood_Light.html, www.weprintcolor.com/moodofcolour.htm, www.webdesignclinic.com/ezine/vli3/mood/, kiradesign.com/ colors.htm, www.icolormyworld.com). Then they can apply their newfound knowledge by testing peers and other people relative to their color and mood sense, creating a database of information. Once the database is developed, students can analyze the data to identify patterns, and then they can suggest interventions that will improve people's moods through color. This activity builds on girls' interest in psychology and their inclination to help people.

See Me

What makes up one's identity? Teenagers are trying to establish their individual identity, navigating through their several interests and roles in life. Students can create digital self-portraits that visually capture their unique combinations of interests. An easy way to start is to scan a photo portrait and then transform it into a line drawing using Photoshop or other visual software. Then students can locate and save images that capture their interests and talents. Each closed area in the line drawing can then be filled with the relevant pictures. Students can analyze their peers' pictures.

Animals and Environment

Visual Inventories

What impact has humankind had on nature? After students discuss possible human–nature interactions, they can collect visual evidence by using cell phone cameras or other digital cameras. They can scout the school or the community and then upload their pictures to a photo-sharing site such as Google Picasa, tagging them to reflect their initial categorization of human–nature interaction. They can then analyze the visual data to uncover possible patterns, such as industrial versus residential interaction, socioeconomic factors, interaction by population demographics, damaging versus beneficial interaction, and so on. Images can also be categorized by cause and effect (e.g., dumping sewage into the water, leading to the death of fish). This activity may be used as an introduction to ecology or as a way to make ecological concepts concrete.

Students can research ways to correct or ameliorate the human impact on nature and incorporate their photos into documents or presentations that call for positive community action. Students can also post visuals, creating hyperlinks to the information they found about their research topic.

Tracking Animals

It can be difficult to track animals, especially in urban settings. BioKids (www.biokids.umich.edu/) enables students to track animals in their natural environments. Students can start by looking at tracks and drawing inferences from the evidence, or they can start with biomes or continents as they locate and analyze tracks with the idea of seeing how tracks reflect animal adaptation to biomes. Students can then use the website to get some ideas of how to preserve endangered species. Students can create web sites and multimedia presentations to targeted audiences to influence them to take action. BioKids also examines common schoolyard animals. Students can develop e-pals from other states or countries to compare the animals around their schools.

Kids Do Ecology

It's never too soon to think about Mother Earth. The National Center for Ecological Analysis and Synthesis provides an outreach program for Santa Barbara (California) fifth graders whereby scientists collaborate with youngsters to gather and analyze data about ecology issues. Its website (www.nceas.ucsb.edu/nceas-web/kids/) has information about biomes, marine animals, and conservation projects. The center also maintains a series of ecological databases that teens can mine in order to test hypotheses about their interdependent environment. This kind of activity can motivate girls to hone their math skills in order to make a difference in their world.

Right On

What rights do animals have? Do they differ by state or country? Do international animal rights exist? Do different kinds of animals have different rights? What impact do animal rights have on people?

Many possible questions exist about animal rights. Students can brainstorm a list and then research animal rights legislation and regulations. They can also examine animal rights organizations. The class can create a grid by region, type of animal, and type of right. Students can role-play a discussion of a controversial animal rights issue (e.g., use of animal products in makeup) in terms of various stakeholders' perspectives on that issue (e.g., manufacturer, teenage consumer, chemist, animal rights activist, and animal keeper). Students can also write to legislators about animal rights or explore other activities that teens could pursue relative to animal rights

Health and Health Care

Advertisements

The intent of advertising is to inform and to persuade. Healthcare providers and public health agencies realize the potential impact of advertising to reach a wide audience. How effective are their advertisements? To what extent are teenage girls influenced? The Center for Media Literacy (www.medialit.org) provides excellent guides for critically analyzing mass media messages. Another good website to gain understanding about visual messages is The People's Choice: Digital Imagery and the Art of Persuasion (www.sedl.org). Here are some guiding questions to consider when examining healthcare advertisements:

1. Who made the advertisement? Was it a public or private entity? Was an outside advertising agency involved, or was it created in-house? Is it possible to determine the role that women had in its production and dissemination?
2. What techniques were used to attract the audience's attention? What images are used, and how? What text is used? Is sound a factor? How are teenage girls portrayed? Each format has its specific approaches: Magazine ads use color and placement (where the ad is located within the issue) to get attention; radio ads try to use an emotional hook through stories and sound effects; television ads take advantage of the in-home experience to develop a sense of intimacy and run the ad during shows that target specific audiences (i.e., compare healthcare public service

announcements shown during *Hannah Montana* and *Murder, She Wrote*).

3. How does the audience experience the advertisement? The ad creator usually has a specific audience in mind. Some ads target one gender: Compare an ad about pregnancy tests with an ad about condoms, even though the underlying issue impacts both males and females. Taking that issue further, most ads about pregnancy tests tend to show females in their twenties and thirties, not teenagers. Do girls and boys experience ads about HIV/AIDS differently? How does the audience react: positively, negatively, neutrally? Is the audience likely to act on the message?

4. What points of view and lifestyles are represented or omitted? Does the health ad sound like a parent or a healthcare professional? Is a teenager's attitude or "voice" apparent—and what does it imply: negative stereotypes or sensitive awareness? Where are teens located: in schools, at home, in neighborhoods, in urban or rural areas, in poor or rich settings, in clean or dirty environments? What are teens doing: consuming, studying, partying, taking risks? What is the sense of relationships: alone, isolated, in couples, in cliques, in crowds, coed or single sex?

From these questions, students can identify which healthcare ads work and why they are effective. With that knowledge, they can suggest ways to improve existing healthcare ads or create ads of their own that are targeted toward their peers.

Telenovelas

Spanish TV soap operas are viewed in many parts of the country these days. Students studying a non-English language can create their own telenovelas (i.e., Latino TV melodramas) about healthcare issues. This format is especially appealing because it often uses exaggerated gestures and emotions to convey ideas and feelings, which facilitates conversational language. Creating a telenovela also requires collaborative discussion and division of work roles, which enables girls to build on their strengths. Students can situate the dramas either at school or in neighborhoods. If a video recorder is not available, students can take still photos to create their story using iMovie or Photo Story; the photos can be sequenced, edited, and narrated with an underlying music track.

Lifeline of Health Care

The class can create two lifetime timelines that show how technology impacts health care for individuals: one for females and one for males. Small groups can focus on one age group (e.g., infant, child, teen, parent, senior citizen), one healthcare provider, or one type of technology. Students can then compare their findings to determine how gender impacts health care, including technology.

Fotonovelas

Using iMac's Comic Life application, students can create comics about almost any healthcare issue: its background, a particular event, personal implications, community efforts. The comic book format facilitates concepts of sequencing, plot development, emphasis of main ideas (usually through frame size), descriptive text, visual information, and combination of story with comic book elements. Students can take original photos, draw original work, or locate existing images. Creating comics collaboratively enables students to divide work and bounce ideas off one another. Fotonovelas (i.e., Latino photo-based graphic novels) are compelling as a way to reframe abstract information into present-day experiences and to particularize a social issue (e.g., HIV/AIDS, eating disorders, runaways). Because social issues can lend themselves to graphic representations (e.g., date rape, domestic violence, gang wars), the project needs to be carefully structured. It might help to discuss ways to represent actions "off camera" or indirectly; alternatively, the "before" and "after" action could be visually portrayed, which helps students understand the conditions and consequences of actions using visuals (e.g., a couple arguing in one frame, a slammed door in the next frame, and a bruised eye in the third frame).

Technically Transforming Health Care

In 2004, President Bush introduced a Health Information Technology Plan (www.whitehouse.gov/infocus/technology/

economic_policy200404/chap3.html). Students should examine this URL carefully; the plan is promoted as part of a technology *economic* policy. What is this plan? What is its background? How is it implemented? What is the government's role? How does economics impact it? These are some questions students might ask as they start to investigate this national plan. Small groups can research one aspect of the plan. Students can generate a list of questions to guide the research in order to facilitate comparisons (e.g., summary of plan, background information, status of implementation, the government's role, economic impact, technology impact, barriers and enhancers, implications for teenagers, implications for families). The class can then share their findings, and create a white paper on the plan: one for teenagers and one for families.

Nano-Nano

Some of the newest technologies in health care cannot be seen with the naked eye. These microscopic machines can enter the body and help healthcare professionals make diagnoses and provide effective interventions. Students can read Isaac Asimov's 1966 book *Fantastic Voyage* or see the movie based on it as a way to start discussion. What is real, what is possible, what is impossible? Then students can research nanotechnology used in health care. Students will quickly find that this technology is controversial and faces many obstacles to general use. The class can list the issues, and small groups can delve into the details of one issue in order to identify barriers and solutions. Another way to divide the class is by application or type of nanotechnology. After they report on their findings, they can reassess *Fantastic Voyage* in terms of its reality or possibilities.

Law

Car Trouble

Most teens dream of driving; it's a sign of freedom and adulthood. Many teens already know that driving has its hazards and potential legal penalties. Are teens are most likely to get into car accidents? States are making it harder for teens to get driver's licenses, and car insurance is usually higher for teen drivers. What about senior citizens? Are they also subjected to tighter regulations and higher costs because they are less able? Students can brainstorm possible car-related situations for which one can be ticketed or fined (which might include the car's physical condition or accidents that happen when the car is parked, such as heat exhaustion if a child or animal is left unattended). Students can then research state and federal laws, noting when age is a factor; they can also compare states in terms of the laws and consequences (each student can research a different state). Based on their findings, students can choose which state is friendliest to teens and to senior citizens. Students can hypothesize about and research why different states have different levels of legal severity (e.g., population density, geography, drinking age, socioeconomic conditions, quantity and availability of police officers).

The Constitution and Teens

Very little mention is made of age in the U.S. Constitution. Students can find those instances as a first activity. However, students are usually aware that they do not have the same rights as adults. Do minors who are *not* students have more rights than students? Are there some rights that apply strictly to college students who are under 21 years of age? Are these rights state- or federally based? What Supreme Court cases have dealt with minors' and students' rights? Have rights changed over time? These are just a few of the possible questions that students might pose when thinking about their rights. Students can brainstorm areas to consider (e.g., drinking, privacy, search and seizure, bearing arms, dress codes, free speech). Then small groups can research a set of rights, constructing an age line that shows how rights change as individuals grow up; branches can be created to show what happens if a student drops out or otherwise changes her status (e.g., marriage, parenthood, military service). The line can also include Supreme Court decisions that have reinforced or altered these rights. Students can then compare the age lines to discover possible patterns. For instance, rights concerning privacy might be stricter than rights concerning drinking. If the class agrees on the dimensions and units for the ageline and prints them out on transparencies, the lines can be superimposed on each other to facilitate comparisons.

CSI Teens

With the advent of crime-scene television shows, the interest in forensics has grown significantly. What are the duties of forensic scientists? What skills and academic preparation are required? Several websites provide accurate information: the Federal Bureau of Investigation (www.fbi.gov), the American Academy of Forensic Scientists (www.aafs.org), and the National Center of Forensic Science (www.ncfs.org). The Girl Scouts have an interest project patch titled "Uncovering the Evidence" (www.studio2B.org/lounge/gs_stuff/ip_evidence.asp), which includes several fun activities that help students learn about forensics (e.g., examining fingerprints, performing DNA extraction in the kitchen, calculating body measurements, analyzing forensics on television). Students can also interview forensic professionals (ideally, videotaping or audiotaping their session in order to archive and share the experience thereafter). Students can research and create a multimedia presentation about one forensic technology "tool" (e.g., camera, PDA, microscope, GPS trackers) or one type of evidence that is examined using technology (e.g., blood, footprints, hair).

Legal Technology

What role does technology play in legal careers? Students can brainstorm a list of legal-related careers. They can then research the skills, academic preparation, and technology aspects of each. Based on their findings, students can create ideal high school and college course plans in order to succeed in each career.

Women in Politics

Women remain underrepresented in the political arena. Half of U.S. lawyers are women, and the majority of politicians are lawyers, yet only 16% of congresspersons are women (Center for American Women and Politics, 2007). Lacking adult role models, girls are less likely to consider politics as a viable career choice. One organization that is trying to address this issue is Mind on the Media. In 2004, it held a conference on women in politics. Some of the recommendations that came out of that meeting, which included teens as well as adult politicians, included:

- Showing women in powerful roles and stances
- Emphasizing women's accomplishments more than their physical appearance and personal details
- Increasing the mass media's coverage of women

Students can research congressional bills, noting their history relative to gender. Alternatively, students can choose women congresspersons, half senators and half representatives, and determine possible trends in bill introductions, sponsors, and voters. Based on their research, students can choose the most effective female congresswoman. Students can then look at media coverage of these women in order to determine whether a correlation exists between coverage and legislative leadership.

Voting According to Gender

To what extent does gender impact voting? Students can research voting patterns relative to issues and then graphically represent voting patterns relative to gender. As an extension, students can research the reasons for gender-linked voting patterns.

Education as a Career

Capturing Technology-Enhanced Teaching

Students usually know who are effective teachers. They probably know who teaches well with technology. Students can videotape these master teachers and then analyze the videotapes, first independently and then with a teacher, to identify those critical events and behaviors that leverage technology well. Based on their analysis, students can then edit the videotape to create a best-practice highlights video or multimedia presentation (using the free application Producer, for instance) that can be shown to a broad audience: aspiring and practicing teachers, the entire school community, and other educators. Those edited sessions can also be digitally rendered and uploaded into a school intranet database for professional development. Sonoma State University's Light Bridge program (lightbridge.sonoma.edu/main/about.html) models this approach to teaching and permits some institutions to submit videos.

Tech Buddy

Teaching is a lifelong learning profession. Because as technology is always changing, teachers have to assimilate new tools constantly. One effective way to learn technology is with a learning buddy; the two can complement each other's skills and ways of knowing. When students and teachers learn together, they can each bring their own generation's perspectives as well as gain greater appreciation for each other's educational roles. This activity works best with same-sex buddy triads: one teacher and two students. Teacher-librarians make great learning buddies because they apply technology across academic subjects and grade levels. Usually the teacher should not be teaching the student at the moment, since it could be construed as unequal treatment by other students; if a student has enjoyed a teacher in the past, that person is a good candidate for this activity.

Tech Personnel and Education

How do technology specialists impact learning? Because technology staff have unique academic and workplace experiences, and may have disparate work duties, their ability and opportunity to influence learning varies greatly. Students probably do not realize these nuances. Students can brainstorm questions to ask technology personnel, and then student pairs can interview different technology specialists, comparing notes afterward. A group-developed cause-and-effect graphic organizer or flowchart can illustrate the impact of each variable.

Assistive Technology

Individuals with special needs can benefit significantly from the effective use of assistive technology. While those technologies are not meant to cure a person's disabilities, they help accommodate that person's needs. Students can research assistive technology and talk with education specialists who work with special-needs youth. Students can also volunteer to help this population. This kind of activity is best done one on one with the child who has special needs, although students may want to buddy up to work with a small set of children with special needs.

Tutoring

One of the best ways to learn about teaching is to tutor a child. This one-on-one experience helps teens learn how to diagnose academic problems and brainstorm possible interventions. Obviously, tutoring needs to be done under the supervision of a master teacher in order to train tutors in the first place and thus optimize the learning experience. Because transportation and time issues can impede tutoring efforts, technology can facilitate interaction. Students can use e-mail, instant messaging, and online chat to mentor youngsters. Skype, a free telecommunications program, lets one use VOIP (voice over internet protocol) and webcams, which makes the mentor feel almost as if she were there.

Student Instructional Design

What's it like to be a teacher? One aspect is designing instruction. Students often find that designing lessons is very different from experiencing a lesson. It requires a deeper understanding of content standards, use of resources, presentation skills, and crafting of guided practice. Incorporating technology as a teaching and learning tool adds another dimension. In this activity, students get to experiment by taking on the teaching role, whether with peers or younger students. They can do this project alone or with another student, but they should collaborate with the classroom teacher or teacher-librarian. Collaborating with a teacher-librarian is an especially useful experience for co-planning and teaching with technology.

Chapter 9

Community-Based Initiatives

Because teenage girls spend significant time outside of school, community agencies and businesses have many opportunities to engage them in technology-rich experiences. In addition, some teenage girls drop out of school, so local entities may be the only way that these girls can connect positively with caring adults. Also unlike schools, community groups can develop a greater variety of programs in terms of content, delivery, and time frame. Individual mentoring and coaching also provide teenage girls with positive role models for technology use (Hull & Schultz, 2002; O'Dell, 2002; Ramnanan, 2001). When community groups coordinate their efforts with one another, including educational institutions, they optimize their impact, particularly for at-risk girls (Gambone et al., 2002).

BUILDING CAPACITY

Because teenage girls are part of the community, it may seem obvious that the community would engage this population. Certainly, girls are prime consumers. Local businesses want to keep young people in the area and hire them, and they often want to make sure that schools prepare them to be productive employees. Moreover, 81% of companies surveyed in 1999 incorporate volunteer activities within their business strategy, knowing that such connections strengthen the community while making good business sense (Girl Scout Research Institute, 2002).

Reaching out to teens seems like a natural connection. However, community members are sometimes unaware of their local teenagers' interests and capabilities, and they may have difficulty connecting with them personally. Business and community efforts need to learn about teens in order to ensure that their resources and time will benefit both parties. Community members can contact youth-serving agencies and educational institutions to discuss teen developmental issues, including gender differences. Only then can businesses and agencies align their goals and strategies with teens'.

Community entities also need to consider several other factors as they start to work with teenagers: availability of resources and support, sustainability of efforts, adequate supervision, confidentiality and privacy issues, insurance, transportation, indemnification issues, parental/guardian permission, labor laws, and sexual harassment laws. Incorporating technology into the partnership equation requires that companies and agencies be comfortable with technology—and sharing it—and be able and willing to train (as well as be trained by) teenage girls in those technologies. In some cases, groups may decide that they do not have the capacity to partner directly with teenage girls, but they can still support community efforts and act as advocates for them.

PROGRAM DEVELOPMENT

Teenage girls need structure at the same time that they want independence; they want to share power, having some say in their collaboration with adults, although they expect adults to serve as safety nets. Girls need concrete goals and strategies, although they want flexibility. Girls need meaningful activities, but they also want to have a good time and make friends. Girls may have a passion for some cause, but they easily change the focus of their commitment (Schoenberg et al., 2002). Understanding these developmental needs helps community entities create age-appropriate programs.

Once a community group decides that it wants to develop a technology-related program for and with teenage girls, it should follow a number of steps:

1. Identify the entity's mission, goals, resources, and strategies. What are its strengths? What does it contribute to the community's well-being? What technology capacity does it have that can help teenage girls?
2. Get to know teenage girls: their characteristics, their backgrounds and experiences, their wants and needs. What are girls' technology experiences and expectations?

3. Align teenage girls' interests with the entity's goals in terms of technology. Possible junctures include: technological expertise, creating products, employment, niche marketing, and communication.
4. Brainstorm ways that outreach efforts can attract and meet the needs of teenage girls. Sample projects include video production, web design, digital storytelling, product or service blogs, product service tutorials, and mentoring programs. Structure programs in such a way that they can be modularized into short-term projects.
5. Prioritize outreach initiatives based on available resources and potential teen participation. Determine if coalitions with other community entities would improve the outcome of the effort.
6. Prepare company or agency personnel. Inform and train all employees as appropriate. Review all policies and procedures that might be impacted by teenage participation; modify practice as needed, and determine what is not negotiable.
7. Promote the program through venues that connect with teenage girls. Ask teens individually to participate. Get recommendations from other community members.
8. Be prepared, and be willing to change and be flexible when working with teenagers. Involve them meaningfully and act on their suggestions as appropriate. Evaluate efforts continuously, and make adjustment as needed. (Farmer, 2005a)

MENTORING AND COACHING

The most effective partnerships between adults and teenage girls are personal, caring, professional, and age-appropriate. Girls want to feel comfortable and safe with adults, and they want to feel that they can trust and depend on adults. Girls want adults to act as adults, not peers. On the other hand, girls probably don't want another parent in their lives; the model of a favorite aunt is a good analogy.

Here are some tips that can help adults mentor and coach teenage girls:

- Get training, and ask for support as needed.
- Know yourself, share yourself, and get to know your mentees.
- Clarify expectations.
- Provide structure and limits; know which are negotiable and which are not.
- Aim for concrete results, and accept short-time commitment.
- Make sure that girls are partners in the endeavor.
- Provide options; offer girls choices, and act on them.
- Provide adequate training, supervision, support, and recognition.
- Act consistently and fairly. If it makes sense to change, tell girls why, and then change after negotiating with the girls.
- Help girls manage their time and document their efforts.
- Help girls connect their community experience with their personal lives and futures.
- Give girls chances to talk out their issues.
- Incorporate social opportunities and skills.
- Be sure that there is an element of fun.
- Know what you can control and what you cannot. Realize that you are not alone.
- Know when to let go.

Regardless of age, whoever interacts with teenage girls needs to respect and appreciate them. Such people need to communicate effectively and listen actively. They need to promote and support high expectations. They should acknowledge and build on teens' interests and needs. They also need to facilitate a sense of an inclusive and accepting community (Young Adult Library Services Association, 2003).

Because teenage girls want and need personal role models that they can identify with, local businesses and agencies should encourage their younger employees to act as mentors and partners with teenagers. Of course, that means that companies need to be aware of Gen X's own priorities: flexibility, fun, and personal fulfillment. Gen Xers may need specialized training and may shy away from long-term commitment, so project-based activities with teenagers can be a good fit. Moreover, Gen Xers are more likely to use technology in such a way that a company's connections with teens might well be strictly virtual (Girl Scout Research Institute, 2002).

COMMUNITY PARTNERS

As noted before, community entities do not have to work alone when partnering with teenage girls. No one group has all the resources and expertise to address all girls' needs, particularly if technology is to be incorporated. As much as possible, community groups should discuss their goals and resources so as to complement one another's strengths as they identify best matches for addressing teenage girls' needs and interests. Possible community groups include:

- Government agencies: libraries, recreation centers, public health centers, educational institutions
- Cultural and entertainment groups: museums, galleries, performance groups, cultural centers
- Social groups
- Faith-based groups
- Private companies and industries
- Professional organizations
- Service and philanthropic organizations
- Local media (Farmer, 2005a)

To build coalitions with the intent of addressing the needs and interests of teenage girls, these groups need to:

- Identify mutual goals
- Identify needed and available resources
- Allocate resources
- Determine strategies
- Coordinate efforts
- Evaluate and follow-up on efforts (Greene & Kochhar-Bryant, 2003)

While building and sustaining a coalition require time, effort, and negotiation, the results will hopefully be worth the investment. The cross-communication alone helps strengthen community and models collaboration for teenagers.

SAMPLE ACTIVITIES

The following learning activities reflect a variety of teenage girls' interests and also link to career opportunities. They take advantage of community resources and informal learning environments to help girls feel connected to their neighborhood and to make a difference locally.

Entertainment

Local Acts

Performers need to promote themselves, even if they have an agent. They need to keep an eye on opportunities, network, and get noticed in order to get an audition and to get a "gig." How does technology fit into these actions? Girls can locate and interview local performers and talent agents to find out technology's role. If there are enough girls, pairs can interview different types of performers and then compare findings. As an extension, girls can create a database of local acts or develop a best advice sheet for teens who want to enter that business.

All the World's a Stage

Viewing a play or movie is a lot different from working behind the scenes. The technical aspect of showing a film or live product has changed over time. Projection booths, lighting, and even the stage itself all involve mechanical and technical equipment. Girls can visit a movie house or theater for a backstage tour. In the process, they can ask what kind of training or preparation is needed for the job. They can also ask about the presence of women in these trades.

Movie Animation

Animated movies reflect a broad range of technical approaches, from the use of cels to computer rendering, from stop-action claymation to pixilation. To start experiencing animated movies as a personal expression, girls can play with Digital Films (www.digitalfilms.com/), which is a simple program that lets the user choose movie elements and create dialog. Girls can also try their hands at creating a short animated movie using stop-action digital cameras and iMovie. As they progress, they can locate and explore free and inexpensive computer animation programs.

Singers

It takes more than a strong pair of lungs to become a professional singer. In fact, few performers these days sing without some kind of technical amplifier. Additionally, most singers need an accompanist (be it live or virtual) in order to perform. What technology is required to produce an album or even a demo recording? Girls can trace the process of producing a recording, noting the role of technology along the way, from choice of song to dissemination of the final product.

Event Planning

Convention halls, fairgrounds, and conference centers all coordinate entertainment events. Event planning is a huge business, and women are increasingly managing these venues. By visiting these sites and talking with event planners or general managers, girls can discover how technology is incorporated throughout the planning and implementation. Girls can take photos to create an event technology timeline. They can also find out what kind of technical knowledge is required of event planners.

Banding Together Online

A single instrument has a much different quality than an ensemble. Ask girls how often they hear solo music. Yet it can be difficult to keep a group together long enough to play well as a team. What about composers who want to hear their music played? They may create arrangements for several instruments but might not themselves be strong players. What if composers or musicians live in a rural area? What chance do they have? With technology, the opportunities are growing. Music can be synthesized. A musician can lay down a track of music, and overlay that with multiple tracks, each played by herself or by others. Increasingly, composers are locating freelance musicians around the world, and collaborating with them online. Girls can research these technology-enhanced music endeavors and do their own music mixing with GarageBand or other software.

Fashion and Beauty

Getting Paid to Shop

Stores hire fashion buyers to buy products to sell. That duty involves keeping current about fashion trends, knowing customer wants, networking with the fashion industry, developing a fashion theme, negotiating with suppliers, and sometimes managing retail sales. How does technology impact such operations? Girls can research the world of fashion buyers and interview them face-to-face or online, noting how technology is incorporated. Girls can also ask what kind of preparation is needed for the job.

Fashion Design Careers and Technology

Nowadays, one can start to learn about fashion design through online courses. Girls can look for jobs online and even interview online. Fashion design work itself involves technology in a number of ways. Girls can create a career flowchart from initial interest to retirement, noting how technology is woven into a fashion designer's life.

Body Techno-Sculpting

Is every model a perfect shape? Hardly. Is the body that one sees on the runway modified by the time it appears on a magazine cover? Frequently. However, nips and tucks don't have to be done surgically; they can be changed through photo editing. Girls can research how technology programs enhance women's images and visit an advertising or magazine agency to see this process in action. Alternatively, they can contact a general photo editor or instructor, asking how their work might be applied to the beauty industry. Girls might also find out how models react to such body techno-sculpting: Does image enhancing help or detract from their careers? Girls can try their own body modification experiments by scanning images and using Photoshop Elements or other photo editing software.

Beauty Competitions

How much technology is involved in beauty competitions? More than what first comes to mind. How does one find out about a beauty competition? How does one apply? What about pictures? Girls can brainstorm all the steps in participating in a beauty competition as well as all the steps in planning and implementing such a competition. Girls can start thinking about the technology of beauty competitions by noting its presence in televised competitions or in movies (e.g., *Little Miss Sunshine, Smile, Miss Firecracker*) and then determining if technological impact has changed over time. Girls can locate other media titles on the Internet Movie Database (www. imdb.com). If possible, girls can contact local beauty contestants or competition planners to learn how technology is incorporated and to compare mass media treatment of beauty competitions with the real event.

Cosmetics

How are cosmetics made? What ingredients are used? How safe are cosmetics? Are they tested? Girls can brainstorm questions about cosmetics and then locate information about their manufacturing and distribution, noting the role of technology along the way, from initial research to product sale. Local stores constitute one part of this process and may have contacts with people who know about this billion-dollar industry. Girls can also have fun finding recipes for making their own cosmetics (e.g., KitchenCosmetics:www.geocities.com/Heartland/Prairie/8088/beauty.html).

Sports and Fitness

The Mechanics of Fitness

Gadgets for body-building and body improvement (e.g., copper bands for thinner waists, electric hats for hair restoration) have been on the market for over a century. Are they effective? Girls can locate mass media advertisements (newspapers, magazines, billboards, television, radio) that claim that their technical gadget (e.g., treadmills, bio-fresh yoga mats, bodywear sensors) produces results. Girls can examine the claims to determine the rigor and reliability of the research methodology used. Next, girls can locate government and medical research about the viability of machines and other technologies for body fitness and enhancement, comparing their methods and findings to those of advertisements. They can also talk with fitness studio and recreation center personnel. In the process, girls should find out how female bodies interact with these machines, in comparison to male bodies. Girls can use their findings to create an advertisement for a specific piece of technology—or to advise against its use.

Exercise Tapes

Youth obesity is a growing concern in the United States. At the same time, physical education and recess time are decreasing as academics are given high priority. How and where are youth supposed to get exercise? One of the options is technology. Television and podcasting can be put to exercise use. Girls can locate and critique existing video and podcast exercise tapes in terms of their interest and fitness quality. For the latter, girls can research exercise training criteria and talk to local trainers; ideally, female adult exercise experts can watch the videos or listen to the podcasts simultaneously to explain the quality of the products. Girls can also videotape their own exercise efforts or choreograph their own exercises (incorporating their own original or public domain music) and tape them. Again, exercise experts can critique them so that improvements can be made. The following website is an example of an online tape critique: www.easytaichi.com/video-evaluation-sample.htm.

Wiis

Nintendo's Wii has become a popular exercise tool. Video simulations of bowling, tennis, and other sports enable one to exercise in front of—and using—the television. So long, couch potato! Girls can work with community agencies to acquire and promote Wiis as a physical fitness program. Even public libraries have held sports events using Wiis.

Giving Everyone a Sporting Chance

Everyone, including individuals with special needs, should be able to enjoy sports and maintain physical fitness. Fortunately, technology has facilitated accommodations and modifications for athletes with disabilities. In fact, one runner with an artificial leg was accused of being advantaged over others because of his limb (the ruling stated that he was not at an advantage, after all) (Longman, 2007). To gather more facts about technological sports equipment, girls can attend Special Olympics competitions or talk with agencies that work with youth who have special needs. As a result, girls may want to volunteer for these groups.

Sports Therapy

Sports medicine and sports therapy have become huge businesses and impact people of all ages. Therapy equipment can be simple or very sophisticated and expensive. Girls can interview athletic trainers and physical therapists to see how incorporating technology affects sports rehabilitation and other physical rehabilitation. Girls can compare treatments for different populations (e.g., girls versus boys, children versus teenagers, sports versus nonsports injuries). Hopefully, girls can experience using some of the technologies or help patients who are being treated.

Media Coverage

Even thought Title IX mandates nondiscrimination in education-based sports, the mass media are not bound by these same regulations. Girls can compare coverage of male and female sports events by different mass media channels. A girl might compare the same event as covered by local television, radio, and newspaper; another girl might compare coverage of a similar sports event involving the opposite sex. Different sports might get different media treatment. After girls analyze the data, they can contact local mass media outlets to interview staff about their sports coverage policies and practices. Ideally, girls could volunteer to cover female sports events themselves for local media.

Personal Advice

Trust Me

Radio and television talk shows often give advice. How much of it is credible? Probably none of those programs would be willing to back up their advice legally; that is, if someone followed their advice and got into trouble, those talk-show hosts cannot be sued. So who should teenage girls believe? Girls can brainstorm criteria for credible public advice and then rate programs. Next, they can contact local social workers and psychologists about these programs, sharing their criteria. Together, girls and adults can recommend valid programs—or ones to avoid.

Can We Talk?

Advertisements for per source advisers often appear in the mass media: from telephone psychics to online sex therapists. It can be very tempting to use these services because girls may feel more anonymous and virtually protected; they can pretend to have certain problems as a way to exploring different issues. How much can girls trust these personal advisers? How much information should they share? Can online personal advisers, such as community hotlines, ever be useful? Girls can talk with community counselors about this issue, devising ways to minimize negative outcomes and promote community-based advising agencies that incorporate technology.

Listen to Your Body

Biofeedback as a self-monitoring approach to health has developed since its inception in the 1960s. For instance, clothing can now be technologically modified to provide information that the wearer can respond to. Nevertheless, biofeedback is controversial. Girls can research new biofeedback tools, linking problems with solutions. They can identify controversial issues and research the basis for claims on both sides: those who use biofeedback and those who oppose it. Girls can contact local health providers to ascertain their stance on the use of biofeedback and learn how to optimize its application. Girls can also focus on the use of biofeedback by teenagers.

Drinking and Technology

The earlier that youth start drinking, the sooner they can become addicted and the more likely it is that they will have a lifelong problem (National Institute on Alcohol Abuse and Alcoholism, 2007). To address this issue, the National Institute on Alcohol Abuse and Alcoholism has developed a series of multimedia information products. Girls can view these documents in terms of their appeal and message; they can also conduct focus groups with their peers to determine which product seems to be the most effective—and why. Girls can then send their findings and recommendations to the institute as a way to information the agency's efforts. Alternatively, girls can create their own public service announcements about underage drinking.

Peer Mentoring

Peer mentoring, particularly among teens, has proven to be a beneficial practice when teens with "street cred" are well trained and supervised by adults. Teens often respond better to their peers than to adults. Finding common time for training and mentoring can be problematic these days, as teens often lead hectic lives. Online training, incorporating asynchronous web tutorials and real-time chat, can ameliorate this situation and expand the number of qualified peer mentors. Girls can explore these possibilities with mentoring adults and create technology-based products to facilitate such online training and possible online mentoring.

In the Pink

Girls think about their breasts as part of their body image, but how many think about breast cancer? Yet most girls know someone who has had breast cancer. Even though most women get breast cancer after menopause, risk factors can be addressed during the teen years as girls create lifelong habits. Girls can research risk factors for breast cancer and then create an interactive quiz or survey giving feedback on ways to improve teens' chances of avoiding or surviving breast cancer. Other possible products that students could create for their peers include lists of facts and myths, a top 10 list of facts, online games, games in quiz format. Another approach is to create publications that help teens cope with relatives or friends who have breast cancer. Here are some good websites to start with: www.4women.gov/FAQ/cbreast.htm, www.youngwomenshealth. org/breast_health.html, www.CancerCare.org, www.PlanetCancer. org. Girls can contact local organizations that address breast cancer with the intent of working with them to produce and disseminate information to youth.

Child Care

Community Technology

Who are the major community stakeholders in children's care: doctors, public health nurses, youth-serving agencies, day-care providers? What technologies do each use? Small groups can each visit a different community after all the teens brainstorm what data they want to collect and how they will collect it (e.g., photos, taped interviews, documented observation). Afterward, teens can compare notes and analyze their data. Using their data, they can create a public service announcement for the community about available health care for children.

Being a Parent Isn't a Disability

How do parents with disabilities take care of their children? What if they can't see or hear the child? What if they have motor limitations? Technology can offer many accommodations for parents with disabilities. An interesting website at which to start this exploration is www.lookingglass.org/publications/pubdetails.php. Girls can visit local hospitals, schools with programs for students with disabilities, and local organizations that support these parents. Girls can test these assistive technologies and share their experiences, thinking in terms of parents' and children's challenges.

Terrifying Toys

Toys are supposed to be fun for children, not harmful. Yet many toys are labeled as unsafe for children under age 3, and most video games are considered inappropriate for little ones. The U.S. Consumer Product Safety Commission makes available several publications about toy safety (www.cpsc.gov/CPSCPUB/PUBS/toy_sfy.html). Girls can read these documents and determine what kinds of criteria are used to test toy safety. They can also research the basis for these criteria. Then they can test toys themselves to see how safe they are. Girls can also visit day-care centers or other locales where preschoolers are supervised (e.g., churches) to survey the safety of the toys made available. Girls might want to modify the criteria and contact the commission about their recommendations.

Early Childhood Education Through Technology

Children are surrounded by technology, be it machines (e.g., refrigerators, televisions, cars) or digital equipment (e.g., cell phones). While any technology—even opening a jar—involves some kind of learning, some technology has explicit learning as its focus. Children who participate in these technology-enhanced learning activities have a head start in school and in lifelong success. What are proven ways that technology can help in early childhood education? Girls can start by exploring the Early Connections website: www.netc.org/earlyconnections/ childcare/curriculum.html. Each girl or small group can concentrate on one aspect of learning: language development, math skills, or motor skills. They can research possible technologies, noting how they are applied, and then visit child-care centers to see if those technologies are available and used appropriately. Girls can learn how to use these technologies and work with children in their application.

Kiddie Kars

Cars are convenient and exciting modes of transportation, but they can be dangerous, especially for children. In response, state and local laws try to safeguard children when it comes to to cars. Girls can brainstorm possible dangers (e.g., air bags, heat exhaustion, access to cars) and identify laws regulating cars and children. Based on their findings, girls can create publications and presentations (e.g., brochures, public service announcements, videos) about child safety and cars. One set of information can target parents and another set can target children.

Day Care as a Business

While relatives and friends still take care of children, day care has become a mainstay for many parents. Nowadays, day care requires much more skill than just watching children; it is a serious business to run. Girls can brainstorm business operations and decisions that have to be made: staff-related issues of hiring, supervision, paying; financial issues of invoicing, expenditures, income tax; facility issues of insurance, bills, safety; and so on. Each of these sets of issues often incorporates technology. Girls can investigate each issue, noting the impact of technology and the need for technical skills. They can research the day-care business and visit local centers. Girls can also compare private and public day-care enterprises in terms of each issue and its incorporation of technology.

Business and Self-Employment

Landing a Job

At some point in their lives, almost all females will need to find a job. How can technology help them? The public library usually has good information about job seeking. A California public library website, jobstar.org/index.php, gives advice on writing resumés, locating available jobs, and applying for them. Girls can create a flowchart about getting a job, from locating a job to the first month on the job. Each step can be annotated with advice and documents to help teens. Special notes can be made about females' experiences or expectations.

Banking on Technology

An urban legend asserts that if a bank system had no electricity for three days, it would go bankrupt. Is that true? To what extent does banking now rely on technology? Can banks determine which demographic group tends to use their technology more: younger customers more than older ones, males more than females? Girls can research basic bank services and costs and develop a list of interview questions. Then they can visit local banks to find out what technological services are available to them at what cost. They can also observe the gender breakdown at the bank in terms of numbers and types of jobs held. Each girl can visit a different bank and then compare notes at the end, including how bank personnel treated them. Are some banks more reliant on technology than others? Are some banks more teen- or female-friendly than others?

Marketing to Teens; Teens as Marketers

The PBS *Frontline* program showed an episode titled "The Merchants of Cool" (www.pbs.org/wgbh/pages/frontline/shows/cool/), which featured teens as popular culture makers and consumers. Girls can explore the website and its links regarding this phenomenon. The website tends to focus on adult perspectives;

girls can interview their peers about teenagers' points of view on teen marketing. In the process, they can investigate the impact of mass media on this audience, both in terms of creating and adopting teen trends. Girls can discover whether gender makes a difference in either case. Girls can also delve deeper, finding out how teen marketers are chosen.

Teen Tech Entrepreneurs

Teenagers are earning over $50,000 as business entrepreneurs. What products or services are they providing? How do they start and proceed? What role does technology play? What demographic groups do successful teen entrepreneurs represent? These are some of the questions that girls can raise and research. For instance, Entrepreneur.com explains the legal issues that underage business starters have to address: www.entrepreneur.com/startingabusiness/startupbasics/legalissues/article55166.html. Girls can also contact youth business programs such as Junior Achievement, MIT's Teen Entrepreneurship Program, and Young Entrepreneurs Alliance for information and advice.

Community Business Organizations

Chambers of Commerce and business groups such as the Lions Club and Rotary Club represent and support local business. Girls can contact these groups to find out how they involve females and teenagers; some business clubs have programs for high schoolers. Girls can find out whether local women's business groups exist and what outreach efforts they make to help mentor teenage girls. The Small Business Administration and the Better Business Bureau represent national business organizations. How do their practices differ from those of local organizations? Girls can brainstorm ways that these organizations can better engage youth and make suggestions to these groups; perhaps they could form an advisory group within the organizations.

Calling All Techies

As companies become more technologically driven, they are having an increasingly difficult time finding and recruiting skilled employees. A smaller percentage of college students are majoring in technology fields such as computer science and engineering. Nevertheless, today's teens who expect to work in technology tend to spend twice as much time on the Internet as their peers and use a wider variety of applications (RoperNOP Technology, 2002). With their day-to-day technology experience, they will have a distinct advantage come hiring time. Industry and government have been developing programs to attract and help prepare teens to enter technology fields. The U.S. government's GEAR-UP initiative, for instance, supports university–business partners who develop meaningful engineering outreach programs for middle and high schoolers. Women in Technology has a Girls in Technology program (www.girlsintechnology.org) to provide support to precollegiate girls. Girls can investigate which local programs support teenage girls who might not otherwise think of technology as part of their future and develop a database of initiatives that can be disseminated to local groups.

Chapter 10

Family-Based Activities

Parents and guardians are children's first teachers, and the two have a natural, emotional connection with each other. Even the simple act of miming parents' actions helps children learn. Likewise, when parents engage in conversation with their children, talking about what they are doing and how they make decisions, they provide opportunities for rich vocabulary and situated language development. When families promote positive attitudes about—and opportunities for—their daughters' technological success, they foster teenagers' self-efficacy and overall high achievement (Bandura, 1997). While the dynamics of family interaction change as children mature, the underlying bond can facilitate family learning and the application of technology as it organically makes sense in daily life.

TODAY'S FAMILIES

What is a family? It is basically a social group of two or more people with a long-term commitment who live together; usually, a family consists of at least one adult and one child. The traditional nuclear family—a male and female married couple with one boy and one girl offspring—describes only 7% of the U.S. population. Nowadays, a family may consist of several adults and children. While one male and one female is the norm for parent pairs, increasingly single-sex couples raise children. Similarly, while single households are usually headed by a female, male-only single parents are becoming more common. The continuing high divorce rate results in many stepfamily configurations, with children coming from either side of the family and other children born from the new union. Other relatives, such as grandparents and aunts/uncles, raise their relatives' offspring because of parental problems or absence. Adoptive families also account for increasing diversity, with parents going to foreign countries to adopt a child in need— or to bypass stringent U.S. procedures. Foster families account for another kind of family, sometimes representing more permanence than serial family situations of live-in coupling and uncoupling. In short, girls grow up in a variety of changing family constellations (Erera, 2001).

Other factors also lead to diverse family values and interactions. People tend to marry later, partly because of financial considerations and partly because acquiring further education delays marriage. Because women today live longer and have fewer children, they have fewer years of caregiving. The majority of mothers enters the marketplace sometime during their children's upbringing, partly because of a desire for a higher standard of living and partly because of unstable economic conditions. For their part, males have taken on more household responsibilities and some even take paternal leave. Gender roles are now less rigid, and couples often have to negotiate their interdependence. Quality of life and self-expression are more important these days (Skolnick & Skolnick, 2006).

Nevertheless, the fundamental concept and value of a family remain. People are basically social creatures who take care of each other. They want to have and raise children, be it to carry on tradition or for self-fulfillment. So, while families have become more diverse in terms of configuration and relationships, they remain the core institution in which most teenage girls develop.

FAMILY DYNAMICS

Parents and guardians have the major responsibility of guiding their children's development and preparing them to become self-sufficient, contributing members of society. Parents and other caring adults bring a lifetime of experiences, a moral compass, and a personal commitment to the betterment of their offspring. Siblings offer fresh perspectives, an eagerness to learn, a need for approval, and peer identification to the family picture. Each person is a unique combination of personality, interests, experiences, and capacities. The interaction of these individuals leads to family dynamics.

Over time, each member of the family gets to know how each

other "works," what "buttons" to push in order to get what one wants. However, as people develop and change, those reactions also change. This renegotiation of family roles spikes when girls enter puberty. Both physical and emotional changes affect females significantly—and usually negatively. Girls are often uncomfortable with their blossoming bodies just as appearance is becoming more important to them. Societal messages and peer influence lead to more rigid expectations and narrower norms, which girls tend to take seriously as they try to establish their own identify. In the process, girls entering puberty are apt to lose their self-confidence and self-esteem. No wonder teenage girls seem to be moody and unpredictable.

At the same time, mothers of teenage girls are likely to be experiencing premenopausal and menopausal changes. Their own bodies are shifting measurably, and their hormones are also readjusting. Some women feel that their sexual lives are slowing down and that they are getting fearfully old. The thought that their daughters will soon be leaving the nest puts added stress on mothers' psyches. Some women who have stayed at home raising children may be facing the need to find outside work, especially if they have to help pay for their children's education. Women who have been out of the educational and paid work loops for more than a decade may rightly feel that they have little chance for meaningful employment. All these changes are frankly scary for women. When they see their daughters growing up and ultimately facing the same challenges, mothers want to both protect and prepare their teenagers.

In any case, the dynamics between family adults and teenage girls need to change in response to these developmental issues. Fortunately, the change can benefit all parties. First of all, parents and guardians have to accept the fact that they are no longer omnipotent; they increasingly need to negotiate decisions and have a more equal relationship, although some expectations can remain nonnegotiable (e.g., drugs, abuse, crime). Girls don't want to be lectured to; they want to be listened to. Girls need more options and need to make more choices as part of the family. Girls want mental and physical space, but they also depend on adults to provide parameters and be available safety nets. Girls sometimes want to avoid problems, but they are appreciative when parents help them figure out how to address and solve problems. Teenage girls are increasingly self-conscious, so they are very sensitive to disrespect and distrust; they still want adult approval, but the motivation is as much for self-confidence as it is for a sense of belonging (Pipher, 1994). If parents and guardians provide a safe and caring environment throughout a young girl's life, offering regular opportunities and support for personal development and competence, then when that girl enters adolescence, she is more likely to have a solid foundation of self-identity and is less likely to feel at a loss.

THE POWER OF TECHNOLOGY

Technology can serve as a method to leverage changing family dynamics and to foster a sense of lifelong learning. Today's teens are digital natives, having grown up in an electronic world, while parents are digital immigrants. It should be acknowledged, however, that this generation was not born with chips in their brains, and many are still not comfortable with a variety of technologies. Likewise, parents and guardians may have been using digital technologies since their own schooldays. Nevertheless, because teenagers usually have more physical dexterity and more available time, they can explore and absorb more technical skills than their adult family members. On the other hand, adults can contextualize technology and understanding its social and ethical implications more fully. Particularly since technology changes constantly, no one person in the family knows everything about technology, so everyone can teach each other, bringing unique contributions to the keyboard.

A family approach to technology offers a concrete way to keep in touch through meaningful activity. It demonstrates parent interest in teenagers and offers a natural way to supervise teens' actions. Each family member may gain new interests or, at least, gain more respect for each other's existing interests and knowledge base. Exploring and using technology as a family offers a concrete activity that meets girls' need to do something and fosters positive risk-taking, which can be difficult for cautious girls. In addition, girls can showcase their own technological skills, acting as experts and being in charge for once in their lives; adults and girls share control. Even when technology does not operate the way intended, adults and teens can help each other cope and problem solve.

Because same-sex modeling is so important for the development of self-efficacy, female adults need to pay particular attention to their attitudes about technology and try to provide a positive openness to technology and lifelong learning; on the other hand, fathers are more likely to reinforce gender stereotypes about technology, so both parents need to support and encourage girls' technological competence (Bussey & Bandura, 1999). This familial acceptance and joint learning helps everyone move to a healthy and more symbiotic relationship. Family members are invested in each other and can benefit from each person's technological competence and contributions.

SAMPLE ACTIVITIES

The following activities help families incorporate technology into their daily lives while empowering their teenage daughters to meet the demands of tomorrow.

Technology as Daily Life

Baby Tech

Technology has certainly become part of baby care. Remote devices monitor a baby's sounds, so parents can monitor the child and, if necessary, rescue the child. Videos targeted to babies (and their parents) such as Baby Einstein are intended to advance a baby's cognitive development (although recent studies state that use of these videos actually impedes vocabulary development). How useful is technology in baby care for families? Small groups can generate charts listing different technologies, each with their advantages and disadvantages. Groups can then compare the charts to determine what and how technologies are used.

Tracking Children

With the increase in reported child abductions and traumatic experiences, family members are increasingly concerned about each other's whereabouts. Cell phones and GPS (global positioning system) devices are gaining acceptance. Some schools are even instituting RFID (radio frequency identification) procedures to track students throughout the day. Some families worry that these tracking devices threaten personal privacy; others find that schools prohibit cell phones and pagers. What action should be taken? Families can discuss how to inform each other about their location and how to keep safe if separated in case of emergencies, such as earthquakes or terrorist attacks. They can research technology-based systems and the school's regulations about them. The family may want to collaborate with other families to modify current school practices relative to tracking children and contacting families using technology.

Healthy Eating

Making sure that teenage girls eat healthful foods can be challenging. Girls are often self-conscious about their bodies, but their hectic lives may make it difficult for them to sit down to a formal meal rather than eat on the go. Using the Internet, families can locate and compare nutritional information about commercial fast foods in order to optimize healthy choices. To help girls learn to prepare food for themselves, families can locate healthy recipes that are quick and easy to prepare. Girls can bookmark or create a family database of recipes. Even locating recipes based on available leftovers can put a new spark into everyday cooking; it's as easy as typing the ingredients and the word "recipe" into a search engine—and it can be a fun activity (What can you make out of peanut butter and leftover turkey? Why, peanut butter turkey rolls, of course: See www.peanut-institute.org/peanutbutterturkeyrolls. html). iParenting provides family tips for healthy eating for teens (recipestoday.com/resources/articles/generationff.htm). California's 2000 fast-food survey findings (www.phi.org/pdf-library/fastfoodsurvey2000.pdf) explain how fast foods affect teen health and make several recommendations that families can implement.

Comparison Shopping

Who has time to comparison shop? And yet convenience can empty the pocketbook quickly. Building on girls' interest in shopping, families can ask their daughters to investigate the relative quality and cost of upcoming major purchases (e.g., entertainment centers, appliances, vehicles). The family can create criteria for judging products as well as locate existing criteria. Girls can list their sources and print out their findings, and the family can negotiate their decisions. Some beginning comparison websites include froogle.com, www.consumerreports.org, shopping.msn. com/content/shp/?ctid=115, www.mysimon.com, and www. econsumer.gov. Families can also compare online consumer sites to determine their relative objectivity and reliability.

Ms. Fix-It

Girls need and want to take care of themselves. Depending on others to make repairs can be time-consuming and expensive. Too often, males play Mr. Fix-It while females play Lady in Distress. Both sexes need to feel confident doing household repairs and operating technology if for no other reason than that the opposite sex might be unavailable or unhealthy at the time. One strategy for learning a skill is to find and follow directions. Increasingly, manuals are available online; one good website, particularly for consumer electronics, is retrevo.com. Another great how-to source, not surprisingly, is www.ehow.com. Families can critique and use the manuals together. They may also find that directions need improvement, or they may discover a better way to do something; www.wikihow.com/ provides a venue for contributing how-to ideas to the public. Girls can also observe and tape the process in order to archive it. Families can also discuss when a repair should be done by an outside expert rather than dealing with it by themselves.

Energy Savings

Family finance is usually the responsibility of adults, and some teenage girls have little comprehension of where the family's money comes from and goes. In some cases, adults are uncomfortable about sharing their financial situation with teenagers. Nevertheless, girls need to learn how to manage expenses when they live independently, and they need to be aware of how their daily behavior can impact the family budget. Utility bills are often a safe venue for discussing family expenses. What is the daily usage rate? How does it compare over the months and years? Girls and their families can find out how much electricity a television or refrigerator uses per hour. What is more electrically draining: entertainment or daily necessities? The energy use of each room can be calculated once the energy use of each item therein is rated. Girls and their families can also research ways to conserve energy use and test a couple of ideas over the month to see if the energy bill declines. Inputting these figures onto a spreadsheet gives girls a chance to sort and calculate expenses and usage. The figures can also be used to make predictions. For instance, if lights were used one hour less, how much money would be saved? Girls can brainstorm ways to calculate energy savings and try them out in real life.

Technology for Fun and Adventure

e-Reading

Can't find time to read? Always on the go? Technology provides great stories to fit your mobile life. Audiobooks can be played on the car's stereo system or downloaded into MP3 players for convenient listening. e-Books can be downloaded onto computer systems to be experienced wherever a laptop is at hand. Families can listen to audiobooks together, or they can experience e-books at their own pace and discuss their reactions to the book as a family. Alternatively, if the family downloads and shares a public domain book in a common cyberspace, members can comment on and annotate the text at any time for everyone to see. Family members can take turns choosing a book, which widens everyone's reading range. Families can also participate in a local family or mother–daughter book club.

Planning Trips

Too often, families plan trips without the benefit of teenage input. As a result, the young person plops herself in the back of the car and tunes out. By jointly deciding on destinations and experiences along the way, families expand the sense of ownership and responsibility for the trip's success. To start with, families can brainstorm places to see or types of experiences to have (e.g., camping, cultural, Xtreme sport, family heritage, photo ops, and so forth). As early as middle school, families should consider taking trips to explore colleges or career options. Girls can serve as the family travel agent, using online mapping programs (e.g., www. mapquest.com and maps.yahoo.com) to get driving directions as well as to explore attractions around the area. They can explore travel advisory sites such as www.letsgo.com and www. lonelyplanet.com to find free and inexpensive things to do; they might also locate travel blogs, although some of these have hidden agendas. Based on their findings, girls can assemble an illustrated trip agenda with accompanying budget range with options for the family to choose from. Don't have time or money to take a real trip? Girls can locate or create an online virtual trip for the family and act as the tour guide.

Games

Online gaming is a hugely popular pastime. However, girls can also use templates to create their own games to play with the family. Here is a starting list of free websites, although parents should review these, since a couple link to more adult content:

- www.any-occasion-party-game.com/free-printable-game. html
- www.gamestemplates.com
- joekid54.tripod.com
- www.powerpointtutorial.org/directory/powerpoint-game-template.html
- www.softplatz.com/software/educational-software/

Cyber Scavenger Hunts

The American Library Association has collected more than 700 fun family websites, accompanied by a parent guide for their use (www.ala.org/gwstemplate.cfm?section=greatwebsites&templat e=/cfapps/gws/default.cfm); many of these will interest teenage girls as well as children. The Internet Public Library's Teen Space (http://www.ipl.org/div/teen/) links to age-appropriate websites and has weekly activities for teens to participate in. Increasingly, public libraries have web pages dedicated to teen interests (yahelp. suffolk.lib.ny.us/virtual.html). Girls can locate fun websites for the family and then develop a family cyber scavenger hunt. Elizabeth Zylstra has created a web-based scavenger hunt tutorial (edtech. boisestate.edu/teki/scavengerhunts.htm) with several examples for girls to look at before they try making their own for their families.

Xtreme Online Sports

Parents and guardians can get nervous when their daugthers start to get interested in Xtreme sports. There are plenty of horror stories about wiping out and crashing. Nevertheless, it can be exhilarating, and some young women can provide positive role models. Here are some youth-serving agencies that show girls in Xtreme sports:

- www.girlsinc.org/gc/page.php?id=8.4
- life.familyeducation.com/sports/role-models/29507.html
- www.allgirlskatejam.com/
- www.xgirlsport.com/
- www.studio2b.org/lounge/gs_stuff/ip_b_xtreme.asp

The last website, from the Girl Scouts, lists a number of activities that teenage girls can do to learn about Xtreme sports and experience them in a safe way.

Family Adventures

The Family Adventure Project (www.familyonabike.org/) offers advice on activities that families can do together, focusing on bikes. Families can connect with other families via this site and share their experiences and photos. This organization also produces a free online newsletter, which follows family adventures in other countries.

Family History

Digital Storytelling

Sure, children can sit in front of the television and see programs that are targeted to their age group. However, the television takes no notice of the child, so viewing is largely passive and disconnected for the youngster. Children love stories, both to hear and to tell. Technology can offer ways to capture those stories for the family in an interactive and personal way. Whether telling a fairy tale or a personal experience, creating digital stories enables everyone to share their voice permanently. The Story Center (www.storycenter. org) defines *digital storytelling* this way: "Digital Storytelling uses digital media to create media-rich stories to tell, to share, and to preserve. Digital stories derive their power through weaving images, music, narrative and voice together, thereby giving deep dimension and vivid color to characters, situations, and insights." Girls and their families can learn about digital storytelling by participating in this WebQuest: faculty.salisbury.edu/~jrbing/ Telling%20a%20Digital%20Story/Telling%20a%20Digital%20 Story.htm. Digital storytelling can be done in many ways; families can brainstorm and implement other ideas as well:

- Capture an oral story using an audiorecording device. Store it on audiotape or cassette, or digitize it for a podcast.
- Videotape an oral story, particularly if the storyteller uses gestures a lot or incorporates artifacts. These may be kept on tape or manipulated into vidcasts.
- Digitize images, and create online storybooks or photo stories using Photo Story (free for PCs) or iMovie (free for Macs).
- Read aloud from a book, recording the reading and making a sound effect each time the page is turned. The stored audio file can be used as a read-along for a child who cannot read but can look at the book.
- Draw pictures for a story and scan them, or create them digitally using a drawing program. Sequence them into an online storybook, narrating or captioning them with a presentation authoring tool such as KidsPix, PowerPoint, or HyperStudio.

• Use family vacation photos as a springboard for an online
  slide show, or create a fictional story that incorporates
  existing photos (e.g., www.csulb.edu/~lfarmer/bangkok/).

Morphing Family Photos

"Will I grow up to look like my relatives?" Teenage girls wonder
about this as they look in the mirror or peruse family albums.
Families can scan family photos and use free or low-cost morphing
software programs to see how images can change. Girls and their
families can test a number of hypotheses:

• Morphing the father's and mother's pictures, girls can
  see if their own features resemble one parent's more than
  another's.
• Morphing parents' and grandparents' pictures, family
  members can see how they might age.
• Morphing relatives' pictures, girls can see if they resemble
  one relative more than another.
• Morphing a boyfriend's picture, girls can predict how
  their children would look; if girls compare the morphing
  result with the morphing of their own parents, they might
  be relieved to see that the outcome might be better than
  expected.

Digital Scrapbooking

Scrapbooking has become a national phenomenon; it can also
get expensive. By using a digital camera or scanning print photos
and other documents, girls can create digital scrapbooks. The
technology allows for more flexibility in layout, the ability to add
comments and links, and the combination of sound and moving
images. Scrapbooking can be a fun family activity, particularly
with older photos, because family members who remember
the context of the photo can talk about their experiences. At the
same time, girls can capture those oral histories on audiotape or
record them directly onto the computer. In either case, the pictures
truly do become alive! DesignerDigitals.com explains how to start

doing digital scrapbooking: www.designerdigitals.com/ecom/
GettingStarted.php. Here are a few digital scrapbooking websites
that the family can explore for ideas and possible hosting:

- www.picaboo.com
- www.digitalscrapbookplace.com/
- www.smilebox.com/designTypes/scrapbooks.jsp
- www.computerscrapbook.com/
- www.allcrafts.net/scrapbook.htm
- 101scrapbookingsecrets.com/tips/Articles/Free_
  Scrapbooking.php

Family Collage

All families own items of personal importance to them:
photographs, mementos, even a piece of cloth might hold special
meaning. One way to capture these memories is to make a collage
of them. However, most people don't want to give up their precious
tokens. Instead, each person can choose items that fit together on
a piece of typing paper. They can then scan the objects using a
computer scanner if possible, but even a color copier can do the job.
Each person arranges the items that show their relationship to one
another, remembering that the item at the layer next to the scanner
surface will show on top. These scanned images themselves can be
photocopied for the extended family to enjoy. Stories can be created
and recorded (onto audio or print files) based on the personal
collages. If the items are scanned on a scanner linked to a computer,
the composition as a whole can be manipulated, or individual items
can be scanned individually to be arranged on an image editing
space. Alternatively, families can amass a set of memorable items,
and each person can rearrange them to fit his or her own memories
and associations.

Connection with Heritage: American Memory

It can be hard for family members to connect if they don't share
common memories. Likewise, new Americans can have difficulty
connecting with cultures within the United States. The Library
of Congress has digitized over a dozen of its special collections

of primary documents about American history (www.loc.gov/ ammem). These digital artifacts include text, photographs and other illustrations, and even film. Families can create visual timelines or historical scrapbooks by locating and sequencing images that either resonate with them or that show cultural trends of the times. The collections can be searched by time, topic, and format. Once images have been gathered, families can talk about each image or write a caption for it.

Acknowledging Parent Contributions

Not everyone's job is glamorous. Sometimes families don't share their work details with their daughters because they think that their work isn't important—or the community does not seem to value their work. In one California community, strawberry pickers constituted a significant portion of the workforce but were not highly regarded. Students researched the local economy in general and the strawberry market in particular. They calculated how much the strawberry workers contributed to the town, not only in money but also in volunteer labor (e.g., helping in schools and churches). Based on their investigation, the students created a multimedia presentation and presented it at a town hall meeting. The students became much more appreciative of their parents' contributions to the community—and the community members themselves also realized the impact of the strawberry workers. Families can explore the social and economic impact of their work with their daughters. The results can be very affirmative.

Advice

School Smarts

One of the best ways that families can help their daughters succeed is to provide positive conditions for learning. Parents and guardians can discuss school smarts with their daughters, identifying current obstacles and finding mutually satisfying solutions. What is the most effective lighting? Can a portable light be used to focus on a study area? Is there a corner for uninterrupted studying, even a makeshift screened-off table after dinner? In particular, parental support and facilitation of technology use can help their children succeed academically (Glennan & Melmed, 1996). What technology can be accessed? Some schools offer family computer workshops and lend or give a working system at the end of the series. Some school libraries lend out laptops. Perhaps a public center such as the local public library can be identified as a locale for public access to technology. Some cell phones include Internet connectivity. Families should also keep in touch with schools in order to know what is going on and what services are available to them. Many schools now have web portals and voice-mail systems that provide information about each child. Teachers are developing their own web pages and telecommunications venues, such as listservs and RSS feeds. Increasingly, parents can look up their children's assignments and grades. Parents can also give feedback to the school about their children's academic experiences. Even families with no Internet access at home may have such access at work; they might also request that schools have longer operating hours or provide open access one or two evenings a week to accommodate families who need technology access. Non-English-speaking families should contact their schools to find out what documents in their primary language and what translation services are available. Perhaps a parent can provide this service to the school on a volunteer or paid basis. Families can also participate in parent organizations, requesting that communication and interaction be provided online. Two valuable organizations that offer online suggestions for parent involvement in education are the National PTA (www.pta.org/programs/stnrdtoc.htm) and the Mid-Continent Research for Education and Learning (www. mcrel.org/SuccessInSight/Default.aspx?tabid=2420). Even the fact that the family is thinking about their daughter's education can demonstrate caring. Of course, families should talk sensitively about their actions; transparent communication helps mitigate a girl's feeling that parents are distrustful or butting into her private life. In addition, since girls tend to underestimate their academic achievement, special effort should be made to objectively point out their capacities (Bussey & Bandura, 1999). In short, parents should demonstrate support, help girls feel OK if they fail and help them get back up, and let them have fun in the process.

Cybersafety Myths and Realities

Young people are increasingly aware of the dangers of telecommunications. They are getting the message: Don't talk to strangers, either in physical space or cyberspace. Many schools prohibit student e-mail transactions. CIPA (Child Internet Protection Act) impacts all federally funded schools and libraries, stating that they must take measures to ensure that youth are protected from pornographic images. Such measures, however, can limit students' need for valid information, including for school assignments. One of CIPA's provisions is that libraries can disable the protective measures if an adult is using the Internet for research purposes. If families go together to public centers to access the Internet, an adult family member can help girls do their homework. At the same time, the adults can see what their daughters are learning at school and become more involved in their education. On a more fundamental level, though, learning how to cope safely in the digital world is a positive lifelong skill. Families can use this opportunity to talk with their daughters about online safety measures. For parents who might not understand the Internet, online resources can provide helpful information. Girls might well be better informed than their parents, so they can exchange idea about what are cybermyths and cyberrealities. In the process of determining cybersafety myth and reality, familes can also look at the source of information to determine the author's bias (e.g., library, parent organization, church, government, and so on). A positive outcome of such discussion can be house cybersafety rules, which might be age- and task-based. Here are some cybersafety websites to explore:

- www.wiredsafety.org/ and its youth sections
- www.wiredkids.org/
- www.teenangels.org/
- www.dmoz.org/Kids_and_Teens/safety_teens.html
- www.netsmartz.org/
- www.ignatius.edu/counseling/docs/cybersafety.pdf
- youthdevelopment.suite101.com/article.cfm/teens_and_ cyber_safety
- www.cybersafety.ca.gov/

- www.lsp.org/safety_tips5.html
- www.safety-council.org/info/child/cyber.html (for a look at a Canadian approach)

Cyberbullying

Bullying predates modern technology. Oog might have threatened Og in Neanderthal days. Parents might remember slam books (i.e., negative gossip notebooks) from their teenage days. However, it can be hard to combat cyberbullying, and the threats and consequences are practically limitless. Nor are girls likely to tell their parents about cyberbullying for several reasons: Parents might embarrass them, make matters worse, or pull the plug on phone and computer use. Furthermore, girls may think that they can take care of it themselves or with the help of their friends. Sometimes they can, and sometimes they can't. Because moral judgment is the last part of the brain to develop, teenagers may still need parental guidance. Of course, family trust is paramount before frank discussion can occur. Nevertheless, discussing the situations of other teens (or hypothetical cases) can be a useful activity and a safety net of discussion and guidance. Adults can learn from teens:

- What they (or other teenage girls) consider to be cyberbullying
- What the consequences are of cyberbullying
- Where they (or other teenage girls) have ever seen/read about instances of cyberbullying
- How they (or other teenage girls) would handle cyberbullying

It would also be important to discuss gender-linked aspects of the above questions. Even if girls play "cool" and say that it would never happen to them, they might be experiencing cyberbullying in real life or might have a friend in that situation. If girls experience cyberbullying (or are tempted to do it themselves) in the future, the past discussion might help them solve their problem. The following websites provide discussion starters:

- www.ncpc.org/cyberbullying?gclid=CMD3jPqBq44CFSNFg Qod6nJtSQ

- www.fightcrime.org/releases.php?id=231
- www.pta.org/archive_article_details_1117639656218.html
- www.kamaron.org/index.php/p/106/t/Cyber-bullying-references-resources-lessons
- www.digitalnative.org/Digital_Safety

When reading about ways to deal with cyberbullying, each family member might rank the effectiveness of the solutions, compare ranks, and discuss the reasons for the differences, if any.

Making Responsible Choices About Drugs

It can be difficult for parents and guardians to tell their children not to use addicting drugs, especially if they themselves use them now or used them as teenagers. Do adults have the right to tell their offspring no when they said—or say—yes themselves? Young people find this stance hypocritical and are bound to challenge such adult edicts. So what is a credible message? One approach is to begin by looking at the facts and advice separately: teens apart from adults. Online quizzes can be fun and nonthreatening, and some of the quiz sites provide valuable information, such as Check Yourself (www.checkyourself.com/?gclid=CPO9meSFq4 4CFRNkYwodWRxgZg), which is a website where teens can check their own behaviors and attitudes. TeensHealth (www.kidshealth. org/teen/drug_alcohol/drugs/know_about_drugs.html) and the National Institute on Drug Abuse (http://teens.drugabuse.gov/) are reputable websites targeted to teens. Adults should become more aware of teens and drugs. These sites target parents:

- www.theantidrug.com/ei/
- www.medicinenet.com/teen_drug_abuse/article.htm
- alcoholism.about.com/od/teens/Teens_and_Substance_ Abuse.htm

Alternatively, teens could examine the websites for adults, and adults could look at websites targeted to teens. Afterward, they can compare notes. It should be noted that many websites for parents are created by residential care facilities, which may be in the business of making a profit by taking in troubled teens. Adults should be wary of such sites and consider them only when all other options fail. At best, such measures are last-ditch possible curatives; they do not focus on preventative ways to support girls as they develop. Likewise, websites about girls and drugs can be very risqué, which, in a way, is an important piece of information.

Want My Advice?

Girls need to test their boundaries and find out who they are as a person. They need to develop self-identity at the same time that they depend on adults as safety nets. Getting and giving advice can be difficult in these circumstances. Parents sometimes treat their teenage daughters as children, sometimes because they do not realize how their children have grown—or because they do realize the changes and may feel uneasy. At the same time, girls may want to give their parents advice but are uncomfortable about such a change in family status. A first step is to learn more about the teen years; here are some websites for parents that also give ideas on advising youth:

- www.education.com/reference/teenyears/?cid=39459
- life.familyeducation.com/parenting/teen/43735.html?detoured=1
- family.go.com/parentpedia/preteen-teen/
- www.byparents-forparents.com/ (this website has some fun quizzes)

Parenting Teens (parentingteens.about.com/) and Time to Talk suggest ways to talk with teens about different issues (www.timetotalk.org/). Teens also need guidance on how to talk to their parents, who may seem more distant or awkward than they were a few years ago. This About site is one of the very few sites targeted to teens: teenadvice.about.com/cs/parentstalkto/ht/parentstalkht.htm. This teen site offers valuable advice to parents as they interact with their own teenagers: www.netsmartz.org/pdf/Teen_Summit_August_2006.pdf.

An interesting activity is to locate websites about teens advising parents and vice versa; the results demonstrate the power imbalance between the two age groups. There are more websites where parents advise teens than where teens advise parents, for instance. A related activity focuses on websites that give advice directly to teens:

- www.grltlk.org/go/ask-katie
- www.teenhelp.org/
- www.teenhealthfx.com/answers/ans_teen.php
- www.teencentral.net/?gclid=CIXu57mWq44CFQcmgAodg HQ7Sg
- www.gravityteen.com/insp.cfm
- www.golivewire.com/teen-advice.cgi

Girls and their parents can compare their perspectives on the quality of the advice. What makes the websites attractive and credible? What lessons can parents learn from these websites? When might these websites be a useful source of help? Part of the discussion can focus on advice to girls as opposed to boys. What differences are noticed? What does this say about advice and girls? Families might explore the concept of starting a teen blog or wiki about advice to parents.

Countering 3M: Mass Media Marketing

Businesses see teenagers as a very profitable target market. Therefore, they spend billions on dollars finding out what teens want. Girls and their families can locate research on marketing to teens. Here are some starter websites:

- www.marketresearch.com/map/cat/1446.html
- www.marketingpilgrim.com/2007/06/marketing-to-teens-social-networking.html
- www.imediaconnection.com/content/12347.asp
- siliconvalley.internet.com/news/article.php/459761

Teens (and their parents) may well be amazed at the attention paid to them. Discussion can address several issues:

- Why are businesses interested in teenagers?
- How accurate is the information?

- What messages do marketers suggest sending?
- What techniques do they suggest using? Are these approaches appealing to teens?
- How are girls and boys differentiated?

As a follow-up activity, girls and their families can look at mass media messages about alcohol. How many are targeted to teens, to women, and specifically to teenage girls? They can also determine if one age group or gender is more likely to be the intended audience. (Note that girls are more likely to be targeted than boys in alcohol advertisements, for instance.) Families can decide how to proceed based on the information they gleaned.

Building Futures Together

Training Parents to Use Technology

The millennial generation is stereotyped as having been born with a computer chip. However, as has been mentioned throughout this book, teenage girls might not feel comfortable with technology. Nevertheless, girls may provide parents with insights about technology use because of its use in schools and other teenage spaces. Technology learning can also be approached as a family activity; local libraries, schools, and recreation centers may conduct family workshops about computer use, for instance. In some cases, businesses may donate computers to families who complete a series of technology workshops.

Sharing Stories About Technology on the Job

Technology comprises a significant part of many jobs, yet parents might not share their technology stories with their children because the technology has become such an integral part of the day, part of the company "wallpaper." Girls can shadow their parents at work, observing what role technology plays. In the process, they might be able to photograph those instances. Afterward, girls can create a map of the facility and attach the appropriate images to the appropriate locations. Ideally, girls can create a mash-up of the two media. As a discussion starter, girls can ask that parent how the job would differ without technology.

Getting Ready for College

College is a big step, not only for teenage girls but also for their families. For some families, the current generation is the first one to go to college. Today, the majority of college students is female, and the gender gap is even wider at the post-baccalaureate level. Nevertheless, preparing for college impacts the entire family and needs to be considered as early as middle school if for no other reason than that girls can plan what courses to take in order to be seriously considered for certain college majors decisions—and can start thinking about how to fund their college and career dreams. Girls and their families can brainstorm about the details of getting ready for college and delineate who has responsibility for the task and who is affected by the task. For example, it might be the responsibility of the girl to seek scholarships, but usually her parents have to fill out the financial forms, and whether she gets the scholarship will certainly impact the whole family one way or another. Girls and their families can create a decision flowchart to capture the myriad decision points and the consequences of decisions. The flowchart can be created with a timeline; alternatively, a Gantt chart can be used to visually plot out projects over time; free templates (e.g., http://www.vertex42.com/ExcelTemplates/excel-gantt-chart.html) can help girls plot out their own futures. Several good books treat this subject, and schools may have college counselors who can help. Suite 101 (www.suite101.com/lesson.cfm/18717/2024/2) has eight "lessons" about college preparation, including parental checklists and offspring.

Building Networks

One of the benefits of technology is its ability to help people network. In fact, social capital constitutes a major factor in career success. Especially for teenage girls who do not explore beyond their neighborhoods or outside their social comfort zone, career-oriented online social networking can open economic doors that would be otherwise closed to them. When telecommunication is combined with face-to-face interactions, the payoff is significant (Warschauer, 2003). As parents and extended family help teenage girls connect with possible mentors or give leads about areas of career interest, they are helping establish a socioeconomic foundation for life.

Families can also find out if their employers have mentorship programs for teenagers, particularly for females. Girls with like interests can help each other with work-oriented connections as well in order to develop a strong social web. Of course, mentoring and other social networks are only as good as the input both parties contribute. Parents can help their daughters learn how to converse in a professional way and ask appropriate questions in order to optimize preprofessional relationships. Parents can also oversee these efforts to make sure they are positive and helpful.

Honing Interviewing Skills

Professional oral communication remains vital in today's workplace. Even though e-mail has shortened some correspondence and modified some writing styles, and instant messaging offers shortcut conversation, speaking face-to-face and remotely (via telephone or videoconferencing) requires self-confidence and poise. Girls and their families can brainstorm the career life of oral communication, from job exploration to interview to phone calls to retirement speeches. Girls can role-play these conversations and have them videotaped for objective assessment. Families may want to pair up, with a girl talking with another adult besides her own parent. Girls can videotape each other, and give feedback. Girls can also role-play by recording messages on telephones to be played back for assessment purposes. Not only can girls see and hear their actions as distinct from their immediate experience, but they can also erase the evidence if it is embarrassing. Ah, that we could all erase those mediocre job interviews!

Politics

Active citizenship is sometimes overlooked among the list of adult responsibilities, yet how each person votes and participates in civil life impacts their lives and the lives of the rest of the nation. It was ultimately one judge who decided who won the presidency in 2000, based on people's voting behaviors. Voting by young adults has declined over the last four decades, and politically disengaged teens are less likely to know their rights or make good use of government services (Center for Information and Research on Civic Learning and Engagement, 2002). Girls are more likely than boys to participate in civic activities and think that they can make a difference. Parents can leverage that interest through modeling positive civic duty: sharing preelection guides and discussing issues, researching candidates' stances on issues that are of interest to girls, attending local caucuses together, bringing their daughters to the voting booth. Girls and their families can also watch television together to discuss politics by critiquing campaign speeches, comparing political advertisements, and analyzing how interest groups lobby. What sections of the Jon Stewart and Stephen Colbert shows are accurate? What are clues about their political stances? How is politics treated by different television channels? Sometimes newscasts have specials that are targeted to young people (e.g., http://www.pbs.org/newshour/extra/speakout/editorial/teens_politics_6-23-06.html). Furthermore, at this point, hundreds of civic-oriented websites target young people. Here are just a few:

- www.chiff.com/home_life/teens-politics.htm
- www.youthoutlook.org
- www.idealist.org
- moveon.org
- www.youthvote.org

Some of these websites have interactive features that allow girls to speak up. Nevertheless, reading and discussing politics and issues isn't enough; girls want to act on their interests. Lauren Long and her mother developed a website to help children become more politically aware (homepage.mac.com/cutepups/Sites/Kidsguide2politics.html). Families can brainstorm how to help support their daughters' civic engagement. Girls might want to videotape government in action, interview government officials, create blogs about civic issues, help a special-interest group, teach younger children about participatory government, babysit children at voting places, and so on. Which would help the world more: a party animal or a political animal?

References

Abram, S. (2007, July). K–12 information literacy: Preparing for the dark side. *Multimedia & Internet@Schools, 25–28.*

Abram, Stephen, & Luther, Judy. (2004, May 1). Born with the chip. *Library Journal, 129*(8), 34–37.

Accreditation Board for Engineering and Technology. (2004). *Criteria definitions.* Baltimore: Accreditation Board for Engineering and Technology.

Agosto, D. (2004, January). Gender, educational technologies, and the school library. *School Libraries Worldwide, 10*(1), 39–51.

American Association of University Women. (1992). *Shortchanging girls, shortchanging America.* Washington, DC: Author.

American Association of University Women. (2000). *Tech-savvy: Educating girls in the new computer age.* Washington, DC: Author.

Asimov, I. (1966). *Fantastic voyage.* New York: Bantam.

Bain, C., & Rice, M. (2006). The influence of gender on attitudes, perceptions, and uses of technology. *Journal of Research on Technology in Education, 39*(2), 119–132.

Baker, F. (2007). *Media literacy clearinghouse.* Columbia, SC: University of South Carolina. Retrieved May 13, 2007, from www.frankbaker.com.

Bandura, A. (1997). *Self efficacy: The exercise of control.* New York: Freeman.

Bauer, J., & Kenton, J. (2005). Technology integration in the schools: Why it isn't happening. *Journal of Technology & Teacher Education, 13*, 519–526.

Baum, J. (2005). Cyberbethics: The new frontier. *TechTrends, 49*(6), 54–55.

Becker, J. (2003). *Digital equity in education and state-level education technology policies: A multi-level analysis.* Unpublished doctoral dissertation, Columbia University, New York.

Belenky, M., Clinchy, B., Goldberger, N., & Tarule, J. (1986). *Women's ways of knowing: The development of self, voice, and mind.* New York: Basic Books.

Beloit College. (2007). *Mindset list.* Beloit, WI: Author. Retrieved September 17, 2007, from www.beloit.edu/~pubaff/mindset/index.php.

Bethea, K. (2002). *Teenage girls in virtual worlds: Do they find online classes meaningful?* Unpublished doctoral dissertation, The University of Wisconsin, Madison.

Binns, J., & Branch, R. (1995). Gender stereotypes computer-clip-art images as an implicit influence in instructional message design. In D. Beauchamp, R. Barden, & R. Griffin (Eds.), *Imagery and visual literacy* (pp. 315–324). Sugar Grove, IL: International Visual Literacy Association.

Black, G. (1995, Fall). *CSMpact for education: Do boys and girls experience education differently?* Rochester, NY: Harris Interactive.

Brooks, J. (1993). *In search of understanding: The case for constructivist classrooms.* Alexandria, VA: Association for Supervision and Curriculum Development.

Brosnan, M. (1998). The impact of psychological gender, gender-related perceptions, significant others, and the introducer of technology upon computer anxiety in students. *Journal of Educational Computing Research, 18,* 63–78.

Brownlow, S., Jacobi, T., & Rogers, M. (2000). Science anxiety as a function of gender and experience. *Sex Roles: A Journal of Research, 42*(1/2), 119–131.

Brunner, C., & Bennett, D. (1997, November). Technology perceptions by gender. *NASSP Bulletin, 81,* 46–51.

Business Software Alliance. (2005). *Fact sheet: The cyber frontier and children.* Washington, DC: Author. Retrieved September 17, 2007, from www.playitcybersafe.com/pdfs/cyberfrontier-children.pdf

Bussey, K., & Bandura, A. (1999). Social cognitive theory of gender development and differentiation. *Psychological Review, 106*(4), 676–713.

California Alliance of of K–18 Partnerships. (2004). *Raising student achievement through effective educational partnerships: Policy and practice.* Long Beach, CA: Author.

California State Department of Education. (2006). DataQuest student technology use survey for California. Sacramento, CA: Author.

Carlson, S. (2005). The net generation goes to college. The Chronicle of Higher Education, 52(7), A34–A37.

Cassell, J., & Jenkins, H. (1998). *From Barbie to Mortal Kombat: Gender and computer games.* Cambridge, MA: MIT Press.

Center for American Women and Politics. (2007). *Women officeholders fact sheets and summaries.* New Brunswick, NJ: Rutgers University. Retrieved August 17, 2007, from www.cawp.rutgers.edu/Facts.html

Center for Information and Research on Civic Learning and Engagement. (2002). *Youth civic engagement.* Washington, DC: Author.

Center for Media Education. (2001). *Teensites.com: A field guide to the new digital landscape.* Washington, DC: Author.

Center for Media Literacy. (2007). *CML medialit kit.* Los Angeles, CA: Author. Retrieved May 13, 2007, from www.medialit.org.bp_mlk.html

Centre for Learning & Performance Technologies. (2007). *Top 100 tools for learning.* Somerset, England: Author. Retrieved September 7, 2007, from www.c4lpt.co.uk/recommended/top100.html.

CEO Forum on Education and Technology. (2001). *School technology and readiness report: Year 4 report.* Washington, DC: Author. Retrieved August 29, 2007, from www.ceoforum.org/downloads/report4.pdf.

Chandler-Olcott, K., & Mahar, D. (2001, November). Considering genre in the digital literacy classroom. *Reading Online, 5*(4), 1.

Chandler-Olcott, K., & Mahar, D. (2003). "Tech-savviness" meets multiliteracies: Exploring adolescent girls' technology-mediated literacy practices. *Reading Research Quarterly, 38*(3), 356–385.

Chao, E. (2002, May). Speech presented at the conference of the Information Technology Association of America, Arlington, VA. Retrieved September 24, 2007, from www.dol.gov/_sec/media/speeches/20020506_ITAA.htm

Children's Defense Fund. (2005). *The state of America's children*. Washington, DC: Author.

Children's Partnership. (2000). *Online content for low-income and underserved Americans*. Santa Monica, CA: Author.

Christensen, R., Knezek, G., & Overall, T. (2005). Transition points for the gender gap in computer enjoyment. *Journal of Research on Technology in Education, 38*(1), 23–37.

Cole, M., & Griffin, P. (Eds.). (1987). *Contextual factors in education: Improving science and mathematics education for minorities and women*. Madison, WI: Wisconsin Center for Education Research, University of Wisconsin–Madison.

College Board. (2006). *Report to the nation*. Princeton, NJ: Author. Retrieved August 29, 2007, from www.collegeboard.com/about/news_info/ap/2006/.

Compaine, B. (Ed.). (2001). *The digital divide: Facing a crisis or creating a myth?* Cambridge, MA: MIT Press.

Consortium for School Networking. (2006). Digital leadership divide. Washington, DC: Author. Retrieved August 17, 2007, from cosn.org/resources/grunwald/digital_leadership_divide.pdf

Coomber, C., Colley, A., Hargreaves, D., & Dorn, L. (1997). The effects of age, gender and computer experience upon computer attitudes. *Educational Research, 39*, 123–133.

Cooper, J., & Weaver, K. (2003). *Gender and computers: Understanding the digital divide*. Mahwah, NJ: Erlbaum.

Crew, H. (1997). Feminist scholarship and theories of adolescent development: Implications for young adult services in libraries. *Journal of Youth Services in Libraries, 10*(4), 405–417.

Daniel, G. (2007, September). Elearning trends in K–12 education. *WWWtools for Education*. Retrieved August 29, 2007, from m.fasfind.com/wwwtools/m/37767.cfm?x=0&rid=37767

Deal, J., & Barker, T. (2003). *Girls will be girls: Raising confident and courageous daughters*. New York: Hyperion.

DeKanter, N. (2005). Gaming redefines interactivity for learning. *TechTrends, 49*(3), 26–31.

Deubel, P. (2006, January). Game on. *T.H.E. Journal*, 30–41.

DeVillar, R., & Faltis, C. (1991). *Computers and cultural diversity: Restructuring for school success*. Albany, NY: State University of New York Press.

Dobosenski, L. (2001). Girls and computer technology: Building skills and improving attitudes through a girls' computer club. *Library Talk, 14*(4), 12–16.

Eckes, T., & Trautner, H. (Eds.). (2000). *The developmental social psychology of gender*. Mahwah, NJ: Erlbaum.

eMarketer. (2005). *Kids and teens: Blurring the line between online and offline*. New York: Author.

Erera, R. (2001). *Family diversity*. Thousand Oaks, CA: Sage.

Fallows, D. (2005). *Search engine users*. Washington, DC: Pew Internet and American Life Project. Retrieved May 12, 2007, from www.pewinternet.org/pdfs/PIP_Searchengine_users.pdf

Farmer, L. (1996). *Informing young women: Gender equity through literacy skills.* Jefferson, NC: McFarland.

Farmer, L. (2005a). *Digital inclusion, teens, and your library.* Westport, CT: Libraries Unlimited.

Farmer, L. (2005b). *Librarians, literacy and the promotion of gender equity.* Jefferson, NC: McFarland.

Farmer, L. (2007). *Collaborating with administrators and educational support staff.* New York: Neal-Schuman.

Federal Interagency Forum on Child and Family Statistics. (2007). *America's children: Key national indicators of well-being, 2007.* Washington, DC: Author. Retrieved September 19, 2007, from www.childstats.gov/americaschildren/highlights.asp

Fine, C. (2001). *Strong, smart, and bold: Empowering girls for life.* New York: Collins.

Fiore, C. (1999). "Women hold up half the sky." Awakening the tech bug in girls. *Learning & Leading with Technology, 26*(5), 10–16.

Fischoff, S., Antonio, J. & Lewis, D. (1998). Favorite films and film genres as a function of race, age, and gender. *Journal of Media Psychology, 3*(1). Retrieved September 19, 2007, from www.calstatela.edu/faculty/sfischo/media3.html

Francis, L., & Katz, Y. (1996). The gender stereotyping of computer use among female undergraduate students in Israel and the relationship with computer-related attributes. *Learning Media and Technology, (22)*2, 79–86.

Furger, R. (2000, May 1). Latinas en ciencia: Making science the technology real for girls. *Edutopia.* Retrieved August 9, 2007, from www.edutopia.org/node/419/print

Gambone, M., Klem, A., & Connell, J. (2002). *Finding out what matters for youth: Testing key links in a community action framework for youth development.* Philadelphia: Youth Development Strategies.

Gee, J. (2003). *What video games have to teach us about learning and literacy.* New York: Palgrave Macmillan.

Gilbert, J. (2007, Winter). Catching the knowledge wave. *Education Canada,* 4–8.

Gilligan, C. (1982). *In a different voice.* Cambridge, MA: Harvard University Press.

Girl Scout Research Institute. (2002). *The community connection: Volunteer trends in a changing world.* New York: Girl Scouts of the U.S.A.

Glennan, T., & Melmed, A. (1996). *Fostering the use of technology.* Washington, DC: RAND Corporation.

Green, C. (2000). *Computing the future: Women, mathematics, and technology. Voices from the pipeline.* Unpublished doctoral dissertation, Northern Illinois University, DeKalb.

Greene, G., & Kochhar-Bryant, C. (2003). *Pathways to successful transition for youth with disabilities.* Upper Saddle River, NJ: Merrill.

Gurian, M., & Henley, P. (2001). *Boys and girls learn differently! A guide for teachers and parents.* San Francisco: Jossey-Bass.

Hackbarth, S. (2001). Changes in primary students' computer literacy as a function of classroom use and gender. *TechTrends, 45*(4), 19–27.

Hafner, K. (2001). *The well: The epic history of the first online community.* New York: Carroll & Graf.

Halpern, D., et al. (2007). *Encouraging girls in math and science*. Washington, DC: Institute of Education Sciences. Retrieved September 22, 2007, from ies. ed.gov/ncee/wwc/pdf/20072003.pdf

Harris, R. (1999). Gender and technology relations in librarianship. *Journal of Education for Library & Information Science, 40*(4), 232–246.

Harris Interactive and Teenage Research Unlimited. (2003). *Born to be wired: New media for a digital generation*. Sunnyvale, CA: Yahoo.

Hayes, E. (2005). Women, video gaming and learning: Beyond stereotypes. *TechTrends, 49*(5), 23–28.

Haynie, W. (2005, April). Where the women are: Research findings on gender issues in technology education. *The Technology Teacher,* 12–15.

Heinich, R. (1996). *Instructional media and technologies for learning*. Upper Saddle River, NJ: Merrill.

Herring, S. (2003). *The handbook of language and gender*. Oxford: Blackwell.

Hobbs, R. (2007). *Reading the media in high school.* New York: Teachers College Press.

Hoffman, L. (2007, August 23). Teens tackle community issues through technology. *My Dorchester,* 1. Retrieved August 17, 2007, from www.scidorchester.org/blogs

Holloway, J. (2000, October). The digital divide. *Educational Leadership, 58,* 90–91.

Hom, M. (2002). *Teacher accommodation of gender learning and problem solving styles in the computer classroom.* Unpublished doctoral dissertation, University of San Francisco.

Horrigan, J. (2007). *A typology of information and communication technology users.* Washington, DC: Pew Internet and American Life Project. Retrieved August 29, 2007, from pewinternet.org/pdfs/PIP_ICT_Typology.pdf

Howe, N., & Strauss, W. (2007). *Millennials go to college: Strategies for a new generation on campus* (2nd ed.). Washington, DC: American Association of Collegiate Registrars.

Hrabowski, F. (2002). *Overcoming the odds: Raising academically successful African American young women.* New York: Oxford University Press.

Hull, G., & Schultz, K. (Eds.). (2002). *School's out! Bridging out-of-school literacies with classroom practice.* New York: Teachers College Press.

International Society for Technology in Education. (2006). *2006 U.S public policy principles and federal objectives.* Washington, DC: Author.

International Society for Technology in Education. (2007). *National educational technology standards for students: The next generation.* Washington, DC: Author. Retrieved August 19, 2007, from www.iste.org/Content/NavigationMenu/NETS/NETSforStudentsStandards2007.doc

International Technology Education Association. (2000). *Standards for technological literacy.* Reston, VA: International Technology Education Association.

Jenkins, H. (1992). *Textual poachers: Television fans & participatory culture.* New York: Routledge.

Jennings, N. (2000). *Across the digital divide: Children, families, and schools in the information society.* Unpublished doctoral dissertation, University of Texas, Austin.

Jenson, J. (1999). *Girls ex machina: A school-based study of gender, culture and technology.* Unpublished doctoral dissertation, Simon Fraser University, Burnaby, Canada.

Johnson, D. (2003). *Learning right from wrong in the digital age: An ethics guide for parents, teachers, librarians, and others who care about computer-using young people.* Worthington, OH: Linworth.

Jones, K. (2000). *Girls and technology: An experimental study to determine the efficacy of using group sessions to change girls' attitudes about technology.* Unpublished doctoral dissertation, University of Alabama, Birmingham.

Kaiser Family Foundation. (2005). *Generation M: Media in the lives of eight to eighteen year olds.* Menlo Park, CA: Author. Retrieved May 19, 2007, from www.kff. org/entmedia/entmedia030905pkg.cfm

Katz, J., Rice, R., & Aspden, P. (2001). The Internet 1995–2000: Access, civic involvement, and social interaction. *American Behavioral Scientist, 45*(3), 405–419.

Keeble, L., & Loader, B. (2001). *Social capital and cyberpower.* London: Routledge.

Kim, J. (2000). *Students' attitudes and perceptions toward technology.* Unpublished doctoral dissertation, Iowa State University, Ames.

Kimmel, M. (2000). *The gendered society.* New York: Oxford University Press.

Koszalka, T. (2002). Technology resources as a mediating factor in career interest development. *Educational Technology & Society, 5*(2), 29–38.

Labaton, V., & Martin, D. (Eds.). (2004). *The fire this time: Young activists and the new feminism.* New York: Anchor Books.

Large, A. (2005). Children, teenagers, and the web. In B. Cronin (Ed.), *Annual review of information science and technology* (pp. 347–392). Medford, NJ: Information Today.

Laskin, D., & O'Neill, K. (1992). *Little girl book.* New York: Ballantine.

LeLoup, J., & Ponterio, B. (2007). *Integrating technology in the foreign language classroom.* Cortland: State University of New York Press. Retrieved August 16, 2007, from www.cortland.edu/flteach/mm-course/clipart2.html

Lemke, C. (2005, Winter). A range of use: Technology in learning. *OnCue,* pp. 12, 21.

Lenhart, A., & Madden, M. (2007). *Social networking websites and teens: An overview.* Washington, DC: Pew Internet & American Life Project. Retrieved August 28, 2007, from www.pewinternet.org/pdfs/PIP_SNS_Data_Memo_Jan_2007.pdf

Lenhart, A., Madden, M., & Hitlin, P. (2005). *Teens & technology.* Washington, DC: Pew Internet and American Life Project. Retrieved May 13, 2007, from www. pewinternet.org/pdfs/PIP_Teens_Tech_July2005web.pdf

Leonard, E. (2003). *Women, technology, and the myth of progress.* Upper Saddle River, NJ: Prentice Hall.

Lepper M., & Malone T. (1987) Intrinsic motivation and instructional effectiveness in computer-based education. In R. Snow & M. Farr (Eds.) *Aptitude, learning and instruction: Cognitive and affective process analysis* (pp. 255–286). Hillsdale, NJ: Erlbaum.

Li, Q. (2006). Computer-mediated communication: A meta-analysis of male and female attitudes and behaviors. *International Journal on e-Learning, 5*(4), 525–570.

Longman, J. (2007, May 15). An amputee sprinter: Is he disabled or too-abled? *The New York Times*, A1, A21.

Lynn, K., Raphael, C., Olefsky, K., & Bachen, C. (2003). Bridging the gender gap in computing. *Journal of Educational Computing Research, 28*(2), 143–162.

Mackoff, B. (1996). *Growing a girl: Seven strategies for raising a strong, spirited daughter.* New York: Dell.

Mann, C. (2001, August). Why 14-year-old Japanese girls rule the world. *Yahoo! Internet Life,* 99–103.

McGillicuddy-De Lisi, A., & De Lisi, R. (Eds.). (2002). *Biology, society, and behavior: The development of sex differences in cognition.* Westport, CT: Ablex.

McGrath, D. (2004, March). Closing the gender gap. *Learning & Leading with Technology, 31*(6), 28–31.

McLester, S. (2007). Technology literacy and the MySpace generation. *Technology & Learning, 27*(8), 17–22.

Media Awareness Network. (2007). *Marketing to teens—Advertising strategies.* Ottawa, Canada: Media Awareness Network. Retrieved September 17, 2007, from www.media-awareness.ca/english/resources/educational/handouts/advertising_marketing/mtt_advertising_strategies.cfm

Mind on the Media. (2004). *Turn beauty inside out 2004.* Northfield, MN: Author. Retrieved August 17, 2007, from www.mindonthemedia.org/TBIO2004.htm

Moir, A., & Jessel, D. (1991). *Brain sex.* New York: Dell.

Morley, J. (2000). Gender differences and distance education. *Journal of Education for Library & Information Science, 48*(1), 13–20.

Nair, S., Flansburg, S., & Hanson, K. (2003). Leveraging the power of diversity to create effective and empowering technology. *Proceedings of the American Society for Information Science and Technology 40*(1), 480–488.

National Center for Educational Statistics. (2004). *The nation's report card.* Washington, DC. Department of Education.

National Center for Education Statistics. (2003). *Internet access in U. S. public schools and classrooms: 1994–2002.* Washington, DC: U.S. Department of Education.

National Institute on Alcohol Abuse and Alcoholism. (2007). Underage drinking research initiative. Bethesda, MD: Author. Retrieved August 24, 2007, from www.niaaa.nih.gov/AboutNIAAA/NIAAASponsoredPrograms/underage.htm.

National Institute on Media and the Family. (2001). *11th annual mediawise® video game report card.* Minneapolis: Author. Retrieved September 20, 2007, from www.mediafamily.org/research/report_vgrc_2006.shtml

National School Boards Association. (2007). *Creating & connecting: Research and guidelines on online social—and educational—networking.* Washington, DC: Author. Retrieved August 24, 2007, from www.nsba.org/site/docs/41400/41340.pdf

National School Boards Foundation. (2000). *Safe and smart: Research and guidelines for children's use of the Internet.* Washington, DC: Author.

National Science Foundation (NSF). (2003). *NSF's program for gender equity in science, technology, engineering and mathematics: A brief retrospective 1993–2001.* Washington, DC: Author. Retrieved September 24, 2007, from www.nsf.gov/pubs/2002/nsf02107/nsf02107.pdf

Negroponte, N. (1995). *Being digital.* New York: Knopf.

Nicholson, K., Hancock, D., & Dahlberg, T. (2007). Preparing teachers and counselors to help under-represented populations embrace the information technology field. *Journal of Technology and Teacher Education, 15*(1), 123–143.

Nonaka, I., & Takeuchi, H. (1995). The knowledge-creating company: How Japanese companies create the dynamics of innovation. New York: Oxford University Press.

North Central Regional Educational Laboratory (NCREL). (2004a). *EnGauge.* Portland, OR: Author.

North Central Regional Educational Laboratory (NCREL). (2004b). *Indicator: Gender equity.* Naperville, IL: Author. Retrieved September 26, 2007, from www.ncrel.org/engauge/framewk/equ/gender/equgenin.htm

Oberman, P. (2002). *Academic help-seeking in the high school computer science classroom: Relationship to motivation, achievement, gender, and ethnicity.* Unpublished doctoral dissertation, Emory University, Atlanta, GA.

O'Dell, K. (2002). *Library materials and services for teen girls.* Greenwood Village, CO: Libraries Unlimited.

Orenstein, P. (1994). *School-girls.* New York: Doubleday.

Ousley, M. (2006). Hope for a more equitable society: Student values and perspectives on race, ethnicity, and gender. *Journal of College & Character, 7*(4), 1–10.

Papert, S. (1980). *Mindstorms.* New York: Basic.

Parsad, B., & Jones, J. (2005). *Internet access in U.S. public schools and classrooms: 1994–2003.* Washington, DC: National Center for Education Statistics.

Partnership for 21st Century Skills. (2004). *Framework for 21st century learning.* Tucson, AZ: Author. Retrieved August 29, 2007, from www.21stcenturyskills. org/index.php?option=com_content&task=view&id=254&Itemid=120

Patrick, S. (2004). Invited commentary: Children, schools, computers, and the Internet: The impact of continued investment in educational technology under NCLB. *Education Statistics Quarterly, 5*(4). Retrieved August 17, 2007, from nces.ed.gov/programs/quarterly/vol_5/5_4/2_4.asp

Pechacek, A. (2007). I can't live without my . . . : Teens' top ten high-tech gadgets and web sites. *Young Adult Library Services, 5* (2), 9–16.

Pellegrini, A., Keto, K., Blatchford, P. & Baines, E. (2002). A short-term longitudinal study of children's playground games across the first year of school: Implications for social competence and adjustment to school. *American Educational Research Journal, 39*(4), 991–1005.

Philbin, M., & Meier, E. (1995, April). A survey of gender and learning styles. *Sex Roles: A Journal of Research.*

Pinkard, N. (2005). How the perceived masculinity and/or femininity of software applications influences students' software preferences. *Journal of Educational Computing Research, 32*(1), 57–78.

Pipher, M. (1994). *Reviving Ophelia: Saving the selves of adolescent girls.* New York: Putnam.

Putallaz, M., & Bierman, K. (Eds.). (2005). *Aggression, antisocial behavior, and violence among girls: A developmental perspective.* New York: Guilford.

Rainie, L. (2006). *Digital natives: How today's youth are different from their "digital immigrant" elders and what that means for libraries.* Washington, DC: Pew Internet and American Life Project. Retrieved September 12, 2007, from www.pewinternet.org/PPF/r/71/presentation_display.asp

Ramnanan, P. (2001). A study on increasing the interest and involvement of females (ages 14 to 18) in technology through skills development and mentoring. Unpublished doctoral dissertation, The Union Institute, Cincinnati.

Rettberg, C. (2006). Teen book discussions go online. *Young Adult Library Services,* 5(1), 35–36.

Rice, F., & Golgin, K. (2004). The adolescent: Development, relationships, and culture. (11th ed.). Boston: Allyn & Bacon.

RoperNOP Technology. (2002). *Mkids international study.* London: United Business Media.

Roschelle, J., Pea, R., Hoadley, C., Gordin, D., & Means, B. (2004, Fall). Changing how and what children learn in school with computer-based technologies. *The Future of Children.*

Rosser, S. (Ed.). (1995). *Teaching the majority: Breaking the gender barrier in science, mathematics, and engineering.* New York: Teachers College Press.

Sadowski, M. (Ed.). (2003). *Adolescents at school: Perspectives on youth, identity, and education.* Cambridge, MA: Harvard University Press.

Salaway, G., Caruso, J., & Nelson, M. (2007). *The ECAR study of undergraduate students and information technology, 2007.* Boulder, CO: EDUCAUSE.

Sanders, J., Koch, J., & Urso, J. (1997). *Gender equity right from the start.* Mahwah, NJ: Erlbaum.

Saul, E. (Ed.). (2004). *Crossing borders in literacy and science instruction: Perspectives on theory and practice.* Newark, DE: International Reading Association.

Scheckelhoff, T. (2006, August/September). Girls & technology: How can we support girls in integrating technologies more fully in their learning? *Library Media Connection,* 52–55.

Schlitz, L. (2007). *Good masters! Sweet ladies!* Cambridge, MA: Candlewick.

Schoenberg, J., et al. (2002). *The ten emerging truths: New directions for girls 11–17.* New York: Girl Scouts of the U.S.A.

Secretary's Commission on Achieving Necessary Skills. (1991). *What work requires of schools: A SCANS report for America 2000.* Washington, DC: Department of Labor.

Sellers, John. (2007). Teen marketing 2.0. *Publisher's Weekly,* 254(35), 27–29.

Silverman, S., & Pritchard, A. M. (1999, September 17). Building their future: Girls and technology education in Connecticut. *Digital Library and Archives.* Retrieved May 13, 2007, from scholar.lib.vt.edu/ejournals/JTE/v7n2/silverman.jte-v7n2.htm

Simpson, E. (2005). What teachers need to know about the video game generation. *Techtrends,* 49(5), 17–22.

Skolnick, A., & Skolnick, J. (2006). *Family in transition* (Rev. ed.) Boston: Allyn & Bacon.

Smith, L. (1999). *The socialization of excelling women with regard to a technology career: Guides and pathtakers.* Unpublished doctoral dissertation, University of Georgia, Athens.

Sousa, D. (2001). *How the brain learns* (2nd ed.). Thousand Oaks, CA: Corwin.

Squire, K. (2006). From content to context: Videogames as designed experience. *Educational Researcher, 35*(8), 19–29.

Stix, G. (2002). Wanted: More mothers of invention. *Scientific American, 286*(6), 34.

Streitmatter, J. (1998). Single-sex classes: Female physics students state their case. *School Science & Mathematics, 98*(7), 369–375.

Technology counts. (2007, March 29). *Education Week.*

The sky's the limit. (2007, July). *Edutopia,* 46–49.

Thom, M. (2001). Balancing the equations: Where are women and girls in science, engineering, and technology? *NASSP Bulletin, 85*(628), 6–19.

Thompson, M. (2005). *Intersecting literacies: Connecting culture, ethnicity and gender.* Unpublished doctoral dissertation, University of Wisconsin, Madison.

Title IX, Education Amendments of 1972. Title 20 U.S.C. Sections 1681–1688. Washington, DC: U.S. Congress.

Turkle, S. (1984). *The second self: Computers and the human spirit.* New York: Simon & Schuster.

Underwood, M. (2003). *Social aggression among girls.* New York: Guilford.

UNICEF. (2003). *Girls' education: Focus on technology.* New York: Author. Retrieved May 13, 2007, from www.unicef.org/girlseducation/index_focus_gender. html

U.S. Department of Labor. (2007). *Statistics.* Washington, DC: U.S. Bureau of Labor. Retrieved August 29, 2007, from ftp://ftp.bls.gov/pub/special.requests/lf/aat9.txt

U.S. Department of Commerce. (2004). *A nation online: Entering the broadband age.* Washington, DC: U. S. Department of Commerce. Retrieved May 13, 2007, from http://www.ntia.doc.gov/ntiahome/dn/

U.S. Department of Education. (2004). *Toward a golden age in American education.* Washington, DC: U.S. Department of Education. Retrieved September 18, 2007, from www.ed.gov/about/offices/list/os/technology/plan/2004/index.html

U.S. Department of Education. (2006). *Gaining early awareness and readiness for undergraduate programs (GEAR UP).* Washington, DC: U.S. Department of Education. Retrieved May 12, 2007, from www.ed.gov/programs/gearup/index.html

U.S. Senate Subcommittee on Science, Technology, and Space of the Committee on Commerce, Science, and Transportation. (2002a). *NASA and education: Hearing before the Subcommittee on Science, Technology, and Space of the Committee on Commerce, Science, and Transportation, United States Senate, One Hundred Seventh Congress, second session, June 19, 2002.* Washington, DC: U.S. Government Printing Office.

U.S. Senate Subcommittee on Science, Technology, and Space of the Committee on Commerce, Science, and Transportation. (2002b). *Women in science and technology: Hearing before the Subcommittee on Science, Technology, and Space of the Committee on Commerce, Science, and Transportation, United States Senate, One Hundred Seventh Congress, second session.* Washington, DC: U.S. Government Printing Office.

Van Eck, R., & the AIM Lab at the University of Memphis. (2006). Using games to promote girls' positive attitudes toward technology. *Innovate Journal, 2*(3). Retrieved September 17, 2007, from innovateonline.info/index.php?view=article&id=209

Volman, M., & Van Eck, E. (2001). Gender equity and information technology in education: The second decade. *Review of Educational Research, 7*(4), 613–634.

Warschauer, M. (2003). *Technology and social inclusion: Rethinking the digital divide.* Cambridge, MA: MIT Press.

Weinman, J., & Haag, P. (1999). Gender equity in cyberspace. *Educational Leadership, 56*(5), 44–49.

Women in Global Science and Technology. (2005). *From the digital divide to digital opportunity: Measuring infostates for development.* Randburg, South Africa: Orbicom.

Yang, J. (2004, December 9). *Asian pop: The gadget gap: Why does all the cool gadget stuff come out of Asia first?* Retrieved August 17, 2007, from www.sfgate.com/cgi-bin/article.cgi?f=/g/archive/2004/12/09/gadgetgap.DTL

Young Adult Library Services Association. (2003). *Young adults deserve the best: Competencies for librarians serving youth.* Chicago: American Library Association.

Zillman, D., & Gan, S. (1997). Musical taste in adolescence. In D. Hargreaves & A. North (Eds.), *The social psychology of music* (pp. 161–187). New York: Oxford University Press.

Index

About the Author

Dr. Lesley Farmer, Professor at California State University Long Beach, coordinates the Librarianship program there. She earned her M.S. in Library Science at the University of North Carolina, Chapel Hill, and received her doctorate in Adult Education from Temple University. Dr. Farmer has worked as a teacher-librarian in K–12 school settings as well as in public, special, and academic libraries. Dr. Farmer chaired the International Association of School Librarianship (IASL) Information Literacy special interest group and serves in leadership roles in the American Library Association and other professional organizations. In 2007, she was chosen as the California Library Association's Member of the Year. A frequent presenter and writer for the profession, Dr. Farmer's most recent books are *The Human Side of Reference and Information Services in Academic Libraries* (2007) and *Collaborating with Administrators and Other Support Staff* (2006). In 2007, she received a Distinguished Scholarly and Academic Achievement Award from her campus. Her research interests include information literacy, collaboration, and educational technology.